Scrap Stripes Afghan,
page 29

STYLISH CROCHET
for the Home™

Table of Contents

Minimalist
Striped
Place Mats,
page 4

Aegean Towel Holder,
page 34

Woodland Mushrooms,
page 13

Ionian Hexagon Tile Throw,
page 43

Moroccan Tile Coasters,
page 38

Ribs Afghan,
page 19

Cozy Blues Blanket

Design by Cozy Nooks Designs

Made using two different weights and fibers of yarn, this blanket creates interest without being complex. You can cozy up with this one on a rainy day and enjoy your relaxing make.

Skill Level
 EASY

Finished Measurements
42 inches wide x 58 inches long, including fringe

Materials
- Lion Brand Vanna's Choice medium (worsted) weight acrylic/rayon yarn (3½ oz/170 yds/100g per skein):
  - 9 skeins #108A dusty blue

- Lion Brand Touch of Alpaca Thick & Quick jumbo (roving) weight acrylic/alpaca yarn (3½ oz/44 yds/100g per skein):
  - 2 skeins #108X moonlight

- Size I/9/5.5mm crochet hook or size needed to obtain gauge
- Size M/N/13/9mm crochet hook
- Tapestry needle
- Stitch markers

Gauge
With size I hook and dusty blue: 9 wide hdc = 4 inches; 9 rows = 4 inches

Pattern Notes
Weave in loose ends as work progresses.

Chain-2 at beginning of row does not count as first stitch unless otherwise stated.

Join with slip stitch as indicated unless otherwise stated.

Scan the code for special pricing on a great yarn substitute.

Special Stitch
Wide half double crochet (wide hdc): Yo, insert hook in between hdc of previous row, yo, pull up a lp, yo and pull through all 3 lps on hook.

Blanket
Row 1: With size I hook and dusty blue, ch 95, hdc in 3rd ch from hook and in each rem ch across, turn. *(93 hdc)*

Row 2: Ch 2 *(see Pattern Notes)*, **wide hdc** *(see Special Stitch)* across, turn.

Rows 3–105: Rep row 2. Fasten off at end of last row.

Border
Join *(see Pattern Notes)* dusty blue in any corner of blanket, ch 1, (sc, ch 1, sc) in same sp, sc evenly sp around, placing (sc, ch 1, sc) in each rem corner, join in beg sc.

Weaving Stripes
Mark rows 16, 18, 25, 53, 81, 88 and 90 with markers. Cut 7 80-inch strands of moonlight. With tapestry needle, weave every other st of marked rows. Start by going up between the border and first st. Tie off each end, leaving a 5-inch tail on both sides. Rep for each marked row.

Optional Moonlight Border
Rnd 1: With size M/N crochet hook, join moonlight in any corner of blanket, ch 1, (sc, ch 1, sc) in same st, sc in every other st around, placing (sc, ch 1, sc) in each rem corner, join in beg sc.

Fringe
Cut 100 7-inch pieces of moonlight. For each knot of fringe, fold 1 piece in half. Insert hook from RS in first sc along 1 short end of blanket; pull folded end through and pull ends through fold. Pull ends to tighten knot. Tie fringe in each sc across each short end. Trim ends even. ●

Minimalist Striped Place Mats

Designs by Britt Schmiesing

These super basic place mats will look great in any color combination.

Skill Level

 BEGINNER

Finished Measurements

19¼ inches wide x 12½ inches tall

Materials

- Premier Yarns Cotton Sprout medium (worsted) weight cotton yarn (3½ oz/180 yds/100g per skein):
    3 skeins #2101-28 bark
    2 skeins #2101-01 cranberry
    1 skein #2101-32 black
- Size H/8/5mm crochet hook or size needed to obtain gauge
- Tapestry needle

Gauge

10 sc = 2½ inches; 20 rows = 4 inches

Exact gauge is not critical for this project.

Pattern Notes

Place Mat 1 can be made with just over 2 skeins of bark. Place Mat 2 will only need 1 skein of bark.

Do not weave in ends. Leave a starting and ending tail of at least 3 inches on each row to create fringe.

Join with slip stitch as indicated unless otherwise stated.

Place Mat 1

Row 1: Leaving a 3-inch tail (see Pattern Notes), with bark, ch 77, fasten off. (77 chs)

Row 2: Working in **back bar of chs** (see illustration), **join** (see Pattern Notes) bark in first ch, ch 1, sc in same ch and each ch across, turn, fasten off. (77 sc)

Back Bar of Chain

Row 3: Join bark in first st, ch 1, sc in same st and each st across, turn, fasten off.

Rows 4–10: Rep row 3.

Rows 11–16: With black, rep row 3.

Rows 17 & 18: With bark, rep row 3.

Rows 19 & 20: With black, rep row 3.

Rows 21–28: Rep [rows 17–20] twice.

Rows 29–32: With bark, rep row 3.

Rows 33–46: Rep [rows 17–20] 3 times, then [rows 17 and 18] once.

Rows 47–52: With black, rep row 3.

Rows 53–62: With bark, rep row 3.

Finishing

Fringe

Tie yarn tails from every 2 rows in an overhand knot up each side of place mat.

Trim fringe to 2 inches.

Place Mat 2

Row 1: Leaving a 3-inch tail *(see Pattern Notes)*, with bark, ch 77, fasten off. *(77 chs)*

Row 2: Working into **back bar of chs** *(see illustration)*, **join** *(see Pattern Notes)* bark in first ch, ch 1, sc in same ch and each ch across, turn, fasten off. *(77 sc)*

Row 3: Join bark in first st, ch 1, sc in same st and each st across, turn, fasten off.

Rows 4–6: Rep row 3.

Rows 7 & 8: With cranberry, rep row 3.

Rows 9 & 10: With bark, rep row 3.

Rows 11–14: Rep [rows 7–10] once.

Rows 15–30: With cranberry, rep row 3.

Rows 31 & 32: With bark, rep row 3.

Rows 33–48: With cranberry, rep row 3.

Rows 49 & 50: With bark, rep row 3.

Rows 51–58: Rep [rows 7–10] twice.

Rows 59–62: With bark, rep row 3.

Finishing

Rep Place Mat 1 finishing. ●

Place Mat 1

Place Mat 2

Sashiko Table Runner

Design by Kathleen Berlew

This artisan table runner combines two meditative needlework techniques—Tunisian crochet and embroidery. The panel is crocheted in Tunisian simple stitch, and then embroidered with a Sashiko-inspired design that's worked from a chart.

Skill Level

 EASY

Finished Measurements

14 inches wide x 51½ inches long

Materials

- Círculo Natural Cotton Maxcolor 4/6 light (light worsted) weight cotton yarn (7 oz/247 yds/200g per ball):
    3 balls #5073 blue
    1 ball #7727 tan
- Size J/10/6mm 14-inch Tunisian crochet hook or interchangeable hook with 12-inch cable or size needed to obtain gauge
- Size G/6/4mm standard crochet hook or size needed to obtain gauge
- Tapestry needle

Gauge

With size J Tunisian hook: 16 sts and 13 rows = 4½ inches in Tss

With size G standard hook: 13 sts = 4½ inches in sc *(border only)*

Take time to check gauge.

Pattern Notes

Weave in loose ends as work progresses.

Each row of Tunisian crochet consists of a forward pass and a return pass with the right side of work always facing.

Special Stitches

Tunisian simple stitch (Tss): With yarn in back, insert hook under front vertical bar from side to side, yo, draw up a lp *(see illustration)*.

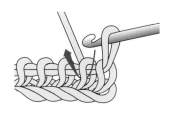

Tunisian Simple Stitch

Return pass: Ch 1 *(see A of illustration)*, [yo, draw through 2 lps on hook *(see B of illustration)*] across. Last lp on hook counts as first lp of next row.

 A

 B

Return Pass

Single crochet bind off (scbo): Insert hook from right to left under front vertical bar of next st, yo, draw up a lp, yo, draw through 2 lps on hook.

Single crochet join (sc join): Place a slip knot on hook, insert hook in indicated st, yo, pull up a lp, yo and draw through both lps on hook.

Table Runner

Row 1 (RS): With Tunisian hook and blue, ch 48, working in **back bar of chs** *(see illustration)*, insert hook in 2nd ch from hook, yo, pull up a lp, keep lp on hook, *insert hook in next ch, yo, pull up a lp, keep lp on hook; rep from * to end of ch. Work **return pass** *(see Special Stitches)*. (48 lps on hook)

Back Bar of Chain

Row 2: Tss *(see Special Stitches)* in each st across to last st, insert hook through both lps of last st, yo, draw lp through. Work return pass.

Rows 3–146: Rep row 2.

Row 147: Scbo *(see Special Stitches)* across. Fasten off.

Scan the code for a photo tutorial for working the Sashiko stitching.

Border

With RS facing, G hook and tan, **sc join** (see Special Stitches) in any st of last row, *sc in each st across to corner, (sc, ch 2, sc) in corner, rotate to work across row ends, sc in each row end across to corner, (sc, ch 2, sc) in corner, rotate to work on underside of foundation ch, rep from * once, sc in each st to end, join with sl st to beg sc. Fasten off.

Embroidery

Refer to **Chart** (see Embroidery Chart) for embroidery details. Each square on chart represents one square on Tunisian crochet fabric.

Thread tapestry needle with a length of tan. Draw needle through several sts on WS of work to secure tail, making sure yarn doesn't show through on RS.

Pull needle to RS at point indicated on chart (at beg of any row of embroidery). Use **running stitch** (see illustration) to embroider horizontal and vertical lines as indicated on Chart. Take care to maintain even tension so embroidery stitches don't pull or sag.

Running Stitch

To finish a strand of yarn, draw tail through several sts on WS to secure.

Finishing

Block table runner facedown on blocking mat to straighten edges and eliminate any curling. ●

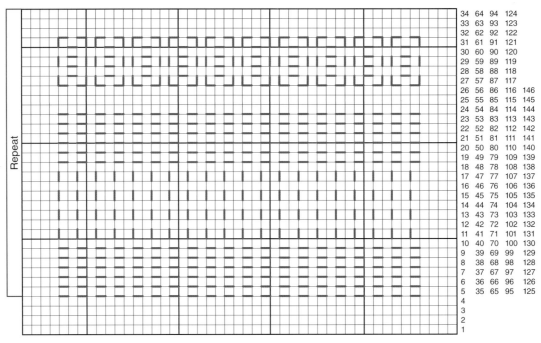

Sashiko Table Runner
Embroidery Chart

KEY
☐ Tss stitch
— Embroidery stitch

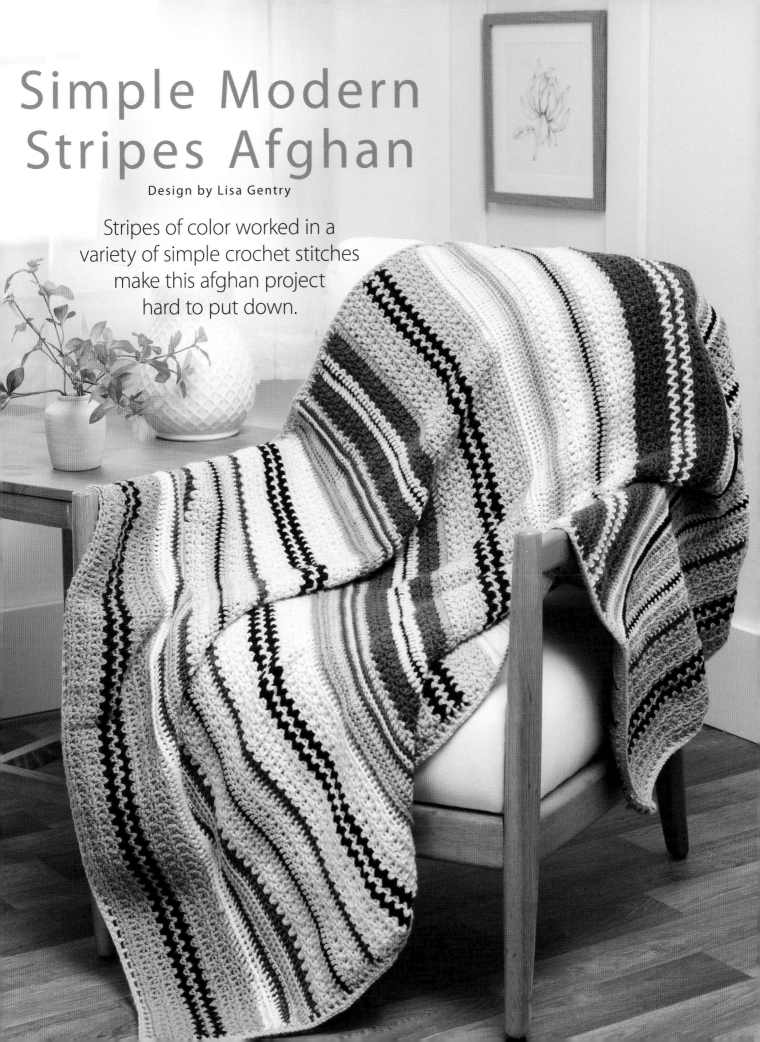

Simple Modern Stripes Afghan

Design by Lisa Gentry

Stripes of color worked in a variety of simple crochet stitches make this afghan project hard to put down.

Skill Level

 **EASY**

Finished Measurements

44 inches wide x 55 inches long

Materials

- Premier Yarns Anti-Pilling Everyday Worsted medium (worsted) weight acrylic yarn (3½ oz/180 yds/100g per skein):
  - 3 skeins each #100-02 cream (C1), #100-72 cloudy day (C3) and #100-89 peach blossom (C6)
  - 2 skeins each #100-86 walnut (C2), #100-55 soft peach (C4) and #100-12 black (C5)
- Size I/9/5.5mm crochet hook or size needed to obtain gauge
- Size H/8/5mm crochet hook or 1 size (0.5mm) smaller than larger hook
- Tapestry needle
- Removable stitch marker

Gauge

With larger hook: 7 V-sts = 4 inches; 10 V-st rows = 4 inches

Pattern Notes

Weave in loose ends as work progresses.

Join with a slip stitch as indicated unless otherwise stated.

Chain-2 at beginning of row counts as first half double crochet unless otherwise stated.

Chain-3 at beginning of row counts as first double crochet unless otherwise stated.

Chain-4 at beginning of round counts as first double crochet and chain-1 space unless otherwise stated.

When working into a V-stitch, work between the posts of the 2 stitches that make up the V-stitch.

After working the main section of the afghan, 13 additional V-stitch rows will be worked in the opposite direction, starting in the bottom of the foundation chain.

Special Stitches

Shallow back post double crochet (sBPdc): Yo, insert hook from back to front and to back again around top section of post *(directly under front and back lps)* of indicated st, yo, pull up a lp *(3 lps on hook)*, [yo and draw through 2 lps on hook] twice.

Double crochet V-stitch (dc V-st): 2 dc in indicated st or sp.

Half double crochet V-stitch (hdc V-st): 2 hdc in indicated st or sp.

Afghan

Main Section

Row 1 (RS): With C1 and using smaller hook, ch 148, dc in 4th ch from hook *(sk chs count as first dc)* and in each ch across, turn. *(146 sts)*

Row 2: Ch 3 *(see Pattern Notes)*, **sBPdc** *(see Special Stitches)* in next and each dc across, fasten off, turn.

Row 3: With smaller hook and RS facing, **join** *(see Pattern Notes)* C2 in first st, ch 3, dc in next and each st across, fasten off. Do not turn.

Row 4 (RS): With larger hook and RS facing, join C3 in first st, ch 1, sc in first and each st across, fasten off, turn.

Row 5: With larger hook and WS facing, working in **front lps** *(see StitchGuide.com)* only, join C6 in first st, ch 1, sc in first and each st across, fasten off, turn.

Row 6: With larger hook and RS facing, working in **back lps** *(see StitchGuide.com)* only, join C3 in first st, ch 1, sc in first and each st across, fasten off. Do not turn.

Row 7 (RS): With smaller hook and RS facing, join C2 in back lp of first st, ch 3, dc in back lp only of next and each st across, fasten off. Do not turn.

Row 8 (RS): With smaller hook and RS facing, join C4 in first st, ch 3, dc in next st, *sk next st, **dc V-st** (see Special Stitches) in next st; rep from * to last 2 sts, dc in last 2 sts, turn. *(71 dc V-sts, 4 dc)*

Row 9: Ch 2 (see Pattern Notes), hdc in next st, **hdc V-st** (see Special Stitches) **in each dc V-st** (see Pattern Notes) across to last 2 sts, hdc in last 2 sts, turn. *(71 hdc V-sts, 4 hdc)*

Row 10: Ch 3, dc in next st, dc V-st in each hdc V-st to last 2 sts, dc in last 2 sts, fasten off. Do not turn. *(71 dc V-sts, 4 dc)*

Row 11 (RS): With smaller hook and RS facing, join C3 in first st, ch 3, treating each dc-V st as 2 dc, dc in next and each dc across, secure working lp with stitch marker and drop working lp from hook. Do not fasten off; do not turn. *(146 sts)*

Row 12 (RS): With larger hook and RS facing, join C5 in first st, ch 1, sc in first and each st across, fasten off, turn.

Row 13: With smaller hook, pick up dropped lp of C3, ch 3, dc in first and each st across, fasten off, turn.

Rows 14–16: Rep rows 8–10. *(71 dc V-sts, 4 dc)*

Row 17 (RS): With smaller hook and RS facing, join C2 in first st, ch 3, treating each dc-V st as 2 dc, dc in next and each dc across, fasten off, turn. *(146 sts)*

Row 18: With smaller hook and WS facing, join C1 in first st, ch 2, hdc in next st, *sk next st, hdc V-st in next st; rep from * to last 2 sts, hdc in last 2 sts, turn. *(71 hdc V-sts, 4 hdc)*

Row 19: Ch 3, dc in next hdc, dc V-st in each hdc V-st to last 2 hdc, dc in last 2 hdc, turn. *(71 dc V-sts, 4 dc)*

Row 20: Ch 2, hdc in next dc, hdc V-st in each dc V-st to last 2 dc, hdc in last 2 sts, turn. *(71 hdc V-sts, 4 hdc)*

Rows 21 & 22: Rep rows 19 and 20, fasten off at end of last row.

Row 23: With smaller hook and RS facing, join C5 in first st, ch 3, dc in next hdc, dc V-st in each hdc V-st to last 2 hdc, dc in last 2 hdc, fasten off, turn. *(71 dc V-sts, 4 dc)*

Row 24: With smaller hook and WS facing, join C1 in first st, ch 2, hdc in next dc, hdc V-st in each dc V-st to last 2 dc, hdc in last 2 sts, turn. *(71 hdc V-sts, 4 hdc)*

Rows 25 & 26: Rep rows 23 and 24.

Rows 27–30: [Rep rows 19 and 20] twice, fasten off at end of last row.

Row 31: With smaller hook and RS facing, join C6 in first st, ch 3, treating each hdc V-st as 2 hdc, dc in next and each hdc across, turn. *(146 sts)*

Rep rows 2–31 in following color sequence:

1 row each: C6, C3, C2, C4, C2, C3; 3 rows C2; 1 row each: C1, C5, C1; 3 rows C2; 1 row C6; 5 rows C3; 1 row each: C5, C3, C5; 5 rows C3; 1 row C1.

Rep rows 2–31 in following color sequence:

1 row each: C1, C4, C3, C4, C3, C4; 3 rows C1; 1 row each: C3, C5, C3; 3 rows C1; 1 row C4; 5 rows C1; 1 row each: C2, C1, C2; 5 rows C1; 1 row C3.

Rep rows 2–30 in following color sequence:

1 row each: C3, C6, C1, C5, C1, C6; 3 rows C3; 1 row each: C1, C5, C1; 3 rows C3; 1 row C2; 5 rows C6; 1 row each: C5, C6, C5; 5 rows C6.

Fasten off.

Additional Rows

Rotate Afghan to **work into bottom** *(see Pattern Notes)* of row 1 of Main Section.

Row 1 (WS): With larger hook, WS facing, and working into bottom of chs, join C6 in first ch, ch 2, hdc in next ch, *sk next ch, hdc V-st in next ch; rep from * to last 2 chs, hdc in last 2 chs, turn. *(71 V-sts, 4 hdc)*

Rep rows 19–30 in following color sequence:

4 rows C6; 1 row each: C5, C6, C5; 5 rows C6. Fasten off.

Edging

Rnd 1 (RS): With smaller hook and RS facing, join C2 in first st, [[**ch 4**—*see Pattern Notes*, dc, ch 1, dc) in first st *(corner)*, *dc in next st, ch 1, sk next st; rep from * to last st, (dc, [ch 1, dc] twice) in last st *(corner)*, working in ends of rows, [dc, ch 1] 96 times across long edge to next corner, working into last row of main section, (dc, [ch 1, dc] twice) in first st *(corner)*, **dc in next st, ch 1, sk next st; rep from ** to last st, (dc, [ch 1, dc] twice) in last st *(corner)*, working in ends of rows, [dc, ch 1] 96 times across long edge to beg corner, join in 3rd ch of beg ch-4. Do not turn.

Rnd 2: With smaller hook, ch 1, (sc, ch 1) in each ch-1 sp around, join in first sc. Fasten off.

Block Afghan to measurements. ●

Woodland Mushrooms

Designs by Fat Lady Crochet

Neutral in tone and simple in design, a bowl full of these woodland mushrooms will add whimsy to your table.

Skill Level

 EASY

Finished Measurements

Pointy Cap Mushroom: 7 inches tall

Wide Cap Mushroom: 5½ inches tall

Materials

- Light (DK) weight yarn: 1¾ oz/50g each beige, cream, peach, dark gray, light gray and pale yellow

 3 LIGHT

- Size C/2/2.75mm crochet hook or size needed to obtain gauge
- Tapestry needle
- Polyester fiberfill
- Locking stitch marker

Gauge

5 sc = 1 inch; 6 rows = 1 inch

Pattern Notes

Caps and Stems are worked separately, then crocheted together.

Work in continuous rounds; do not join or turn unless otherwise stated. Place stitch marker at beginning of round and move up as each round is completed.

Weave in ends as work progresses.

All pieces worked in rounds begin with 2 chains and indicated number of single crochet worked in 2nd chain. If desired, begin instead with **slip ring** (see illustration), chain 1 and work stitches in ring. Pull gently on beginning tail to close ring after round 1 is completed.

Stuff as indicated, but not so stuffing shows through stitches.

Join with slip stitch as indicated unless otherwise stated.

Special Stitches

Increase (inc): 2 sc in indicated st.

Single crochet join (sc join): Place a slip knot on

4" end

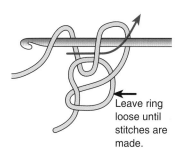

Leave ring loose until stitches are made.

Slip Ring

hook, insert hook in indicated st, yo, pull up a lp, yo, draw through both lps on hook.

Mushrooms

Pointy Cap Mushroom

Stem

Rnd 1: With beige, **ch 2, 9 sc in 2nd ch from hook** *(see Pattern Notes)*. **Do not join, place marker in first st** *(see Pattern Notes)*. *(9 sts)*

Rnd 2: Inc *(see Special Stitches)* in each st around. *(18 sts)*

Rnd 3: Working in **back lps** *(see StitchGuide.com)*, sc in each st around.

Rnds 4–12: Sc in each st around.

Rnd 13: [Sc in next 4 sts, **sc dec** *(see StitchGuide.com)* in next 2 sts] around. *(15 sts)*

Rnds 14–17: Sc in each st around.

Rnd 18: [Sc in next 3 sts, sc dec in next 2 sts] around. *(12 sts)*

Stuff *(see Pattern Notes)* firmly and continue to stuff as work progresses.

Rnds 19–30: Sc in each st around, **change color** *(see StitchGuide.com)* to cream in last st of last rnd.

Rnd 31: Inc in each st around. *(24 sts)*

Rnd 32: Sc in each st around.

Rnd 33: Inc in each st around. *(48 sts)*

Rnd 34: [Sc in next 3 sts, inc in next st] around. *(60 sts)*

Rnd 35: Working in **front lps** *(see StitchGuide.com)*, sc in each st around, **join** *(see Pattern Notes)* in beg sc. Fasten off.

Cap

Rnd 1: With peach, ch 2, 6 sc in 2nd ch from hook. Place marker in first st. *(6 sts)*

Rnd 2: [Sc in next st, inc in next st] around. *(9 sts)*

Rnd 3: Sc in each st around.

Rnd 4: [Sc in next 2 sts, inc in next st] around. *(12 sts)*

Rnd 5: Sc in each st around.

Rnd 6: [Sc in next 3 sts, inc in next st] around. *(15 sts)*

Rnd 7: [Sc in next 4 sts, inc in next st] around. *(18 sts)*

Rnd 8: Sc in each st around.

Rnd 9: [Sc in next st, inc in next st] around. *(27 sts)*

Rnd 10: Sc in each st around.

Rnd 11: [Sc in next 2 sts, inc in next st] around. *(36 sts)*

Rnds 12 & 13: Sc in each st around.

Rnd 14: [Sc in next 3 sts, inc in next st] around. *(45 sts)*

Rnd 15: [Sc in next 15 sts, inc in next st] around. *(48 sts)*

Rnd 16: [Sc in next 3 sts, inc in next st] around. *(60 sts)*

Rnds 17 & 18: Sc in each st around.

Rnd 19: Holding Cap and Stem tog and working through both thicknesses of Cap and in back lps of rnd 34 of Stem, sc in each st around, **stuffing** *(see Pattern Notes)* Cap firmly just before completion, join in beg sc. Fasten off.

Finishing

With dark gray, embroider long **straight stitches** *(see illustration)* across underside of Cap as shown in photo.

Straight Stitch

Flat Top Mushroom

Stem

Rnd 1: With beige, **ch 2, 9 sc in 2nd ch from hook** *(see Pattern Notes)*. **Do not join, place marker in first st** *(see Pattern Notes)*. *(9 sts)*

Rnd 2: Inc *(see Special Stitches)* in each st around. *(18 sts)*

Rnd 3: [Sc in next st, inc in next st] around. *(27 sts)*

Rnd 4: Working in **back lps** *(see StitchGuide.com)*, sc in each st around.

Rnds 5–9: Sc in each st around.

Rnd 10: [Sc in next 7 sts, **sc dec** *(see StitchGuide.com)* in next 2 sts] around. *(24 sts)*

Rnds 11–14: Sc in each st around.

Stuff *(see Pattern Notes)* firmly and continue to stuff as work progresses.

Rnd 15: [Sc in next 6 sts, sc dec in next 2 sts] around. *(21 sts)*

Rnds 16–23: Sc in each st around.

Rnd 24: [Sc in next 5 sts, sc dec in next 2 sts] around. *(18 sts)*

Rnd 25: Sc in each st around, **change color** *(see StitchGuide.com)* in last st to dark gray.

Rnd 26: Sc in each st around.

Rnd 27A: Ch 2 *(counts as first dc)*, working in **front lps** *(see StitchGuide.com)*, dc in each st around, join in top of beg ch-2. Fasten off.

Rnd 27B: Working in back lps of rnd 26, **sc join** *(see Special Stitches)* dark gray in first sc, sc in each st around. *(18 sts)*

Rnd 28: Sc in each st around.

Rnd 29: Inc in each st around. *(36 sts)*

Rnd 30: [Sc in next 3 sts, inc in next st] around. *(45 sts)*

Rnd 31: [Sc in next 4 sts, inc in next st] around. *(54 sts)*

Rnd 32: [Sc in next 5 sts, inc in next st] around. *(63 sts)*

Rnd 33: [Sc in next 6 sts, inc in next st] around. *(72 sts)*

Rnds 34 & 35: Sc in each st around, join in beg sc at end of last rnd. Fasten off.

Cap

Rnds 1–3: With pale yellow, work same as Stem rnds 1–3.

Rnd 4: Sc in each st around.

Rnd 5: [Sc in next 2 sts, inc in next st] around. *(36 sts)*

Rnd 6: [Sc in next 3 sts, inc in next st] around. *(45 sts)*

Rnd 7: Sc in each st around.

Rnd 8: [Sc in next 4 sts, inc in next st] around. *(54 sts)*

Rnd 9: Sc in each st around.

Rnd 10: [Sc in next 5 sts, inc in next st] around. *(63 sts)*

Rnd 11: [Sc in next 6 sts, inc in next st] around. *(72 sts)*

Rnd 12: Sc in each st around. Do not fasten off, drop lp from hook and place on marker.

With light gray and tapestry needle, embroider **French knots** *(see illustration)* randomly over Cap.

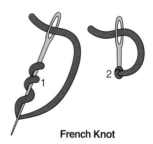

French Knot

Rnd 13: Pick up lp and place on hook, holding Cap and Stem tog and working through both thicknesses, sc in each st around, **stuffing** *(see Pattern Notes)* Cap lightly just before completion, join in beg sc. Fasten off. ●

Hygge Bobble Rug

Design by Margret Willson

Make your home cozy and stylish at the same time with this amazing rug. This sturdy, beautiful rug is made by alternating rounds of a soft bulky-weight yarn and an acrylic bulky-weight yarn.

Skill Level

 INTERMEDIATE

Finished Measurements

48 inches in diameter, including fringe; 42 inches in diameter, excluding fringe

Materials

- Red Heart Hygge bulky (chunky) weight acrylic/nylon yarn (5 oz/132 yds/141g per skein):

  5 BULKY

  2 skeins each #8319 rust, #8339 cloud, #8568 slate blue, #8631 aloe, #8633 forest and #8724 powder
- Red Heart With Love Chunky bulky (chunky) weight acrylic yarn (5 oz/171 yds/141g per skein):

  3 skeins #1401 pewter
- Size J/10/6mm crochet hook or size needed to obtain gauge
- Size L/11/8mm crochet hook for fringe
- Tapestry needle

Gauge

Rnds 1–4 = 4½ inches

Pattern Notes

Weave in loose ends as work progresses.

Join with slip stitch as indicated unless otherwise stated.

All rounds are worked with right side facing unless otherwise stated.

Chain-3 at beginning of round counts as first double crochet unless otherwise stated.

Chain-4 at beginning of round counts as first double crochet plus chain-1 space.

Chain-5 at beginning of round counts as first double crochet plus chain-2 space.

Special Stitches

Single crochet join (sc join): Place slip knot on hook, insert hook in indicated st, yo and pull up a lp, yo and draw through both lps on hook.

V-stitch (V-st): Working in front of ch sp, dc in next sk st 2 rows below, sc in ch sp, dc in same sk st 2 rows below.

Beginning cluster (beg cl): Sc join *(see Special Stitches)* in indicated st, ch 2, [yo, insert hook in same st, yo, draw lp through, yo, draw lp through 2 lps on hook] 3 times, yo, draw lp through all 4 lps on hook.

Cluster (cl): [Yo, insert hook in indicated st, yo, draw lp through, yo, draw through 2 lps on hook] 4 times, yo, draw lp through all 5 lps on hook.

Beginning shell (beg shell): Join in indicated st, ch 3, 2 dc in same st.

Shell: 3 dc in indicated st.

Treble cluster (tr cl): [Yo twice, insert hook in indicated st, yo, draw lp through, (yo, draw through 2 lps on hook) twice] 3 times, yo, draw lp through all 4 lps on hook.

Rug

Rnd 1: With pewter, ch 4, 9 dc in 4th ch from hook *(beg 3 sk chs count as a dc)*, **join** *(see Pattern Notes)* in 3rd ch of beg 3 sk chs. *(10 dc)*

Rnd 2: Ch 3 *(see Pattern Notes)*, dc in same st as join, 2 dc in each st around, join in 3rd ch of beg ch-3. Fasten off. *(20 dc)*

Rnd 3 (WS): With WS facing and with rust, work **beg cl** *(see Special Stitches)* in any st, *ch 3, sk next st**, **cl** *(see Special Stitches)* in next st, rep from * around, ending last rep at **, join in top of beg cl. Fasten off. *(10 cls, 10 ch-3 sps)*

Rnd 4 (RS): Sc join forest in any cl, ***V-st** *(see Special Stitches)* in next sk st 2 rows below**, sc in next cl, rep from * around, ending last rep at **, join in first sc. Fasten off. *(10 V-sts, 10 sc)*

Rnd 5: Join pewter in any dc, **ch 5** *(see Pattern Notes)*, sk next sc, *dc in next dc, ch 2, sk next sc, rep from * around, join in 3rd ch of beg ch-5. Fasten off. *(20 dc, 20 ch-2 sps)*

Rnd 6: Sc join slate blue in same st as joining, *V-st in next sk sc 2 rows below, sc in next dc, working in front of next ch-2 sp, dc in next sk sc 2 rows below**, sc in next dc, rep from * around, ending last rep at **, join in first sc. Fasten off. *(10 V-sts, 10 dc, 20 sc)*

Rnd 7: With cloud, work **beg shell** *(see Special Stitches)* in sc at center of any V-st, *sk next 2 sts, **shell** *(see Special Stitches)* in next dc**, sk next 2 sts, shell in next sc, rep from * around, ending last rep at **, join in 3rd ch of beg ch-3. Fasten off. *(20 shells)*

Rnd 8: Sc join aloe in first dc of any shell, sc in next 2 dc, *working in front of previous row, dc in next sk sc 2 rows below**, sc in next 3 dc, rep from * around, ending last rep at **, join in first sc. Fasten off. *(20 dc, 60 sc)*

Rnd 9: Join pewter in first sc after any dc, **ch 4** *(see Pattern Notes)*, *sk next sc, dc in next sc, ch 1, sk next dc**, dc in next sc, ch 1, rep from * around, ending last rep at **, join in 3rd ch of beg ch-4. Fasten off. *(40 dc, 40 ch-1 sps)*

Rnd 10: Sc join powder in same st as joining, *dc in next sk sc 2 rows below, sc in next dc, **tr cl** *(see Special Stitches)* in next sk dc 2 rows below**, sc in next dc, rep from * around, ending last rep at **, join. Fasten off. *(20 tr cls, 20 dc, 40 sc)*

Rnd 11: Join pewter in any st, ch 3, dc in each st around, join in 3rd ch of beg ch-3. Fasten off. *(80 dc)*

Rnd 12 (WS): With rust, work beg cl in any st, *ch 2, sk next st**, cl in next st, rep from * around, ending last rep at **, join in top of beg cl. Fasten off. *(40 cls, 40 ch-2 sps)*

Rnd 13 (RS): Sc join forest in any cl, *working over next ch-2 sp, dc in next sk st**, sc in next cl, rep from * around, ending last rep at **, join in first sc. Fasten off. *(40 dc, 40 sc)*

Rnd 14: Join pewter in any sc, ch 5, sk next dc, *dc in next sc, ch 2, sk next dc, rep from * around, join in 3rd ch of beg ch-5. Fasten off. *(40 dc, 40 ch-2 sps)*

Rnd 15: Rep rnd 6. *(20 V-sts, 20 dc, 40 sc)*

Rnd 16: Rep rnd 7. *(40 shells)*

Rnd 17: Rep rnd 8. *(40 dc, 120 sc)*

Rnd 18: Rep rnd 9. *(80 dc, 80 ch-1 sps)*

Rnd 19: Rep rnd 10. *(40 tr cls, 40 dc, 80 sc)*

Rnd 20: Join pewter in any tr cl, ch 3, *dc in next st, **dc dec** *(see StitchGuide.com)* in next 2 sts**, dc in next st, rep from * around, ending last rep at **, join in 3rd ch of beg ch-3. Fasten off. *(120 dc)*

Rnd 21: Rep rnd 12. *(60 cls, 60 ch-2 sps)*

Rnd 22: Rep rnd 13. *(60 dc, 60 sc)*

Rnd 23: Rep rnd 14. *(60 dc, 60 ch-2 sps)*

Rnd 24: Rep rnd 6. *(30 V-sts, 30 dc, 60 sc)*

Rnd 25: Rep rnd 7. *(60 shells)*

Rnd 26: Rep rnd 8. *(60 dc, 180 sc)*

Rnd 27: Rep rnd 9. *(120 dc, 120 ch-1 sps)*

Rnd 28: Rep rnd 10. (60 tr cls, 60 dc, 120 sc)

Rnd 29: Join pewter in any tr cl, ch 3, *dc dec in next 2 sts**, dc in next st, rep from * around, ending last rep at **, join in 3rd ch of beg ch-3. Fasten off. *(160 sts)*

Rnd 30: Rep rnd 12. *(80 cls, 80 ch-2 sps)*

Rnd 31: Rep rnd 13. *(80 dc, 80 sc)*

Rnd 32: Rep rnd 14. *(80 dc, 80 ch-2 sps)*

Rnd 33: Rep rnd 6. *(40 V-sts, 40 dc, 80 sc)*

Rnd 34: Rep rnd 7. *(80 shells)*

Rnd 35: Rep rnd 8. *(80 dc, 240 sc)*

Rnd 36: Rep rnd 9. *(160 dc, 160 ch-1 sps)*

Rnd 37: Rep rnd 10. *(80 tr cls, 80 dc, 160 sc)*

Rnd 38: Join pewter in any tr cl, ch 3, *[dc dec in next 2 sts] twice, dc in next st, dc dec in next 2 sts**, dc in next st, rep from * around, ending last rep at **, join in 3rd ch of beg ch-3. Fasten off. *(200 dc)*

Rnd 39: Rep rnd 12. *(100 cls, 100 ch-2 sps)*

Rnd 40: Rep rnd 13. *(100 dc, 100 sc)*

Rnd 41: Rep rnd 14. *(100 dc, 100 ch-2 sps)*

Rnd 42: Rep rnd 6. *(50 V-sts, 50 dc, 100 sc)*

Rnd 43: Rep rnd 7. *(100 shells)*

Rnd 44: Rep rnd 8. *(100 dc, 300 sc)*

Rnd 45: Rep rnd 9. *(200 dc, 200 ch-1 sps)*

Rnd 46: Rep rnd 10. *(100 tr cls, 100 dc, 200 sc)*

Rnd 47: Join pewter in any tr cl, ch 3, *[dc dec in next 2 sts] twice**, dc in next st, rep from * around, ending last rep at **, join in 3rd ch of beg ch-3. *(240 dc)*

Rnd 48: Rep rnd 12. *(120 cls, 120 ch-2 sps)*

Rnd 49: Rep rnd 13. *(120 dc, 120 sc)*

Rnd 50: Sc join pewter in any st, sc in each rem st around, join in first sc. Fasten off. *(240 sc)*

Fringe

Choosing colors at random, cut 3 7-inch strands for each fringe. Fold strands in half. Insert hook in any sc, draw folded end through. Draw ends through fold and tighten knot.

Rep in each sc around. Trim fringe evenly to 3 inches long. ●

Ribs Afghan

Design by Melissa Leapman

Post stitches and shell stitches create an easy to memorize textured pattern on this versatile fall afghan.

Skill Level

 INTERMEDIATE

Finished Measurements

54 inches wide x 71 inches long, excluding fringe

Materials

- Premier Anti-Pilling Everyday Medley medium (worsted) weight acrylic yarn (3½ oz/219 yds/100g per skein):
  - 17 skeins #1132-09 rust
- Size H/8/5mm crochet hook or size needed to obtain gauge
- Tapestry needle

Gauge

7 sts = 2 inches; 9 dc rows = 5 inches

Pattern Notes

Weave in loose ends as work progresses.

Chain-3 at beginning of row counts as first double crochet unless otherwise indicated.

Special Stitch

Shell: Ch 3, 3 dc around post of last dc made.

Afghan

Row 1: Ch 235, dc in 4th ch from hook, dc in next 6 chs, [ch 1, sk next 3 chs, dc in next ch, **shell** *(see Special Stitch)*, ch 1, sk next 3 chs, dc in next 7 ch] across to last ch, dc in last ch, turn. *(121 dc, 16 shells)*

Row 2: Ch 3 *(see Pattern Notes)*, *[{**bpdc**—*see StitchGuide.com* around next st, dc in next 2 sts} 2 times, bpdc around next st], ch 3, sc in ch-3 sp of next shell, ch 3; rep from * 15 more times; rep between [ ], dc in last st, turn.

Row 3: Ch 3, *[{**fpdc**—*see StitchGuide.com* around next st, dc in next 2 sts} 2 times, fpdc around next st], ch 1, dc in next sc, shell, ch 1; rep from * 15 more times; rep between [ ], dc in last st, turn.

Rows 4–128: Rep rows 2 and 3 alternately, ending with row 2. At end of last row, fasten off.

Fringe

For each fringe, cut 9 strands each 14 inches long. With all strands held tog, fold in half, insert hook in ch sp, draw fold through, draw all loose ends through fold, tighten. Trim ends.

Evenly space 51 fringe across each short end of afghan. ●

Scan the code for a great deal on 2-packs of yarn perfect for this afghan.

Textured Pumpkin

Design by Dana Hogan of Day's Crochet

Spruce up your fall home decor with this gourd-geous boho pumpkin!

Skill Level

 INTERMEDIATE

Finished Measurements

6 inches wide x 5 inches tall, unstuffed and measured flat

Materials

- Círculo Yarns Natural Cotton 4/6 light (light worsted) weight Brazilian virgin cotton yarn (24¾ oz/865 yds/700g per ball):
    1 ball #20 cream
- Size 7/4.5mm crochet hook or size needed to obtain gauge
- Tapestry needle
- Polyester fiberfill
- Small length of white pipe cleaner
- 15mm wood beads: 5
- 20mm wood beads: 3
- Hot-glue gun and hot-glue sticks
- 4-inch-wide piece of cardboard

Gauge

12 sc = 4 inches; 15 rows = 4 inches

Pattern Notes

Weave in loose ends as work progresses.

Join with slip stitch as indicated unless otherwise stated.

For larger Pumpkin, add foundation chains in multiples of 4. Finished height should measure 1 inch shorter than width, measured flat.

Special Stitch

Front post double crochet decrease (fpdc dec):
*Yo, insert hook from front to back to front again around post of first indicated st, yo, pull up a lp, yo and draw through 2 lps *(2 lps on hook)*, rep from * around next indicated st *(3 lps on hook)*, yo and draw through all 3 lps.

Note: *You may be instructed to sk sts as legs of fpdc dec are worked.*

Pumpkin

Rnd 1: Leaving a long tail for sewing, ch 48, **join** *(see Pattern Notes)* in first ch to form a ring, ch 1, hdc in same ch as join and in each ch around, join in beg hdc. *(48 hdc)*

Rnd 2: Ch 1, **bphdc** *(see StitchGuide.com)* around same st as join, **fphdc** *(see StitchGuide.com)* around next st, [bphdc around next st, fphdc around next st] around, join in beg hdc.

Rnd 3: Ch 1, hdc in each st around, join in beg hdc.

Rnd 4: Ch 1, hdc in first 2 sts, working first leg around first fphdc, sk next fphdc and working last leg around next fphdc, **fpdc dec** *(see Special Stitch)* 2 rows below, sk next st *(behind hook)*, [hdc in next 3 sts, working first leg around last fphdc worked, sk next fphdc, and working last leg around next fphdc, fpdc dec 2 rows below, sk next st *(behind hook)*] around, working last leg around first fphdc worked *(completes first fpdc dec)*, hdc in last st, join in beg hdc. *(12 fpdc dec, 36 hdc)*

Rnd 5: Rep rnd 3.

Rnd 6: Ch 1, hdc in first 2 sts, fpdc dec around first fpdc dec and next fpdc dec 2 rnds below, sk next st *(behind hook)*, [hdc in next 3 sts, fpdc dec around last fpdc dec worked and next fpdc dec 2 rnds below, sk next st *(behind hook)*] around to last st, hdc in last st. *(12 fpdc dec, 36 hdc)*

Rnds 7–23: Rep rnds 5 and 6.

Rnd 24: Rep rnd 5.

Rnd 25: Rep rnd 2.

Rnd 26: Ch 1, sc in first st, [sk next st, sc in next st] around to last st, sk last st, join in beg sc. Leaving a long tail, fasten off. *(24 sc)*

Assembly & Finishing

Weave beg tail through sts of rnd 1 and pull gently to close. Secure and leave rem tail for later use.

Lightly stuff Pumpkin evenly; do not overstuff so that stuffing is visible between sts. Weave end tail

Scan the code to learn how to create this pumpkin.

through **back lps** *(see StitchGuide.com)* of rnd 26, pull gently to close. Secure tail, then thread on needle and push through Pumpkin and out bottom hole. Tie both tails tog tightly to bring top and bottom tog. Knot several times and weave tails through Pumpkin.

Stem

Fold pipe cleaner in half. Slide 1 each 15mm and 20mm beads on pipe cleaner and glue 15mm bead and top of pipe cleaner tog. Apply glue to opposite end and place Stem on top indentation.

Tassels

Cut 2 15-inch strands. Holding strands tog, tie as 1 strand unevenly around base of Stem so tails are of different lengths. With 20mm bead between 2 15mm beads, slide 3 beads on each pair of tails. Do not trim end tails.

Wrap yarn around cardboard 30 times. Cut across bottom edge and separate strands into 2 hanks of 15 strands.

For each Tassel, fold hank in half. Separate end tails below beads and tie tightly through fold. Thread end tails through center of Tassel and trim all strands evenly to desired length.

Optional: *To create "neck," before trimming strands, cut 6-inch strand for each Tassel. Wind around Tassel 1 inch below bead, pull tightly and knot. Thread ends through center of Tassel.* ●

Hanging Produce Bags

Designs by Debra Arch

Free up space and add style to your kitchen with these super stretchy produce bags. They work up quickly so you can make several in different colors to adorn the room.

Skill Level

 EASY

Finished Measurements

Large Bag: approximately 14 inches long x 6¾ inches wide, excluding hanging loop and without stretching

Slender Bag: approximately 12 inches long x 3¾ inches wide, excluding hanging loop and without stretching

Materials

- Bernat Maker Home Dec bulky (chunky) weight cotton/nylon yarn (8¾ oz/317 yds/250g per skein):
    1 skein each #11005 aqua and
      #11001 woodberry
- Size L/11/8mm crochet hook or size needed to obtain gauge
- 1-inch diameter button (1 per bag)
- 6–8mm wood beads in desired shapes and colors: 16–22 beads per bag
- Stitch markers: 2
- Tapestry needle
- 12-inch square of cardboard (for tassels)

Gauge

In Large Bag pattern: 3 dc cls and 2 ch-5 sps = 4 inches; 4 rows = 4 inches

Pattern Notes

The larger of these super stretchy produce bags holds up to 3 pounds of produce while the slender bag can be customized to desired length to hold smaller amounts of veggies stacked vertically. Both bags' tassels are accented with wood beads and feature unique button tops which can be unbuttoned from bag to remove tassels before washing.

1 skein has enough yarn to make both bags.

Join with slip stitch as indicated unless otherwise stated. Do not join at end of rounds unless otherwise stated.

Work only into chain spaces, skipping all stitches, unless otherwise stated.

Weave in loose ends as work progresses.

Special Stitches

Chain 8 and place marker (ch 8 pm): Ch 8, place a stitch marker in 3rd ch *(from base)* of 8 chs made. Counts as tr and ch-5 sp.

Double crochet cluster (dc cl): Yo, insert hook in indicated st or sp, yo, pull up a lp, yo, draw through 2 lps on hook, yo, insert hook in same st or sp, yo, pull up a lp, yo, draw through 2 lps on hook *(3 lps on hook)*, yo, draw through all 3 lps on hook.

Double crochet cluster join (dc cl join): Place a slip knot on hook, yo, insert hook in indicated st or sp, yo, pull up a lp, yo, draw through 2 lps on hook, yo, insert hook in same st or sp, yo, pull up a lp, yo, draw through 2 lps on hook *(3 lps on hook)*, yo, draw through all 3 lps on hook.

Single crochet join (sc join): Place a slip knot on hook, insert hook in indicated st, yo, pull up a lp, yo and draw through both lps on hook.

Bags

Large Bag

Top

Row 1: With aqua, ch 10, **join** *(see Pattern Notes)* in first ch to form a ring *(hanging lp)*, **ch 8 pm**, *(see Special Stitches)*, **dc cl** *(see Special Stitches)* in ring, ch 5, tr in ring, turn. *(2 tr, 1 dc cl, 2 ch-5 sps)*

Row 2: Ch 8 pm, dc cl **in first ch-5 sp** *(see Pattern Notes)*, ch 5, dc cl in next ch-5 sp, ch 5, tr in marked ch and remove marker, turn. *(2 tr, 2 dc cls, 3 ch-5 sps)*

Row 3: Ch 8 pm, dc cl in first ch-5 sp, [ch 5, dc cl in next ch-5 sp] across, ch 5, tr in marked ch and remove marker, turn. *(2 tr, 3 dc cls, 4 ch-5 sps)*

Rows 4–8: [Rep row 3] 5 times. *(2 tr, 8 dc cls, 9 ch-5 sps)*

Rnd 9: Rep row 3, do not turn at end of row, join in marked ch at beg of rnd and remove marker. Fasten off. *(2 tr, 9 dc cls, 10 ch-5 sps)*

Bottom

Note: Bottom of bag is worked in rnds. Beg of rnd shifts in first rnd.

Rnd 1: Sk next 3 ch-5 sps, **dc cl join** *(see Special Stitches)* in next ch-5 sp, [ch 5, dc cl in next ch-5 sp] 9 times, ch 5, join in top of beg dc cl. *(10 dc cls, 10 ch-5 sps)*

Rnd 2: Sl st in first 3 chs of first ch-5 sp, ch 3 *(counts as dc)*, dc in same sp, [ch 5, dc cl in next ch-5 sp] 9 times, ch 5, sk beg ch-3, join in next dc. *(2 dc, 9 dc cls, 10 ch-5 sps)*

Rnd 3: Rep rnd 2.

Rnd 4: Sl st in first 3 chs of first ch-5 sp, ch 3 *(counts as dc)*, [dc in next ch-5 sp] 9 times, join to top of beg ch-3. Fasten off, leaving a 12-inch tail. *(10 dc)*

Using tapestry needle, weave tail in and out of dc of last rnd, pull yarn until opening is about ½-inch in diameter *(buttonhole for tassel accent)*, knot yarn ends tightly to secure and cut away excess.

Edging

Rnd 1: With RS facing, and treating all tr around top opening as ch sps, **sc join** *(see Special Stitches)* aqua in first ch sp after hanging lp, 2 sc in same sp, 3 sc in each sp around to hanging lp, 15 sc in hanging lp, join in **front lp** *(see StitchGuide.com)* of beg sc, turn. *(69 sc)*

Rnd 2: Ch 1, sl st in each st around, join in first sl st. Fasten off. *(69 sl sts)*

Slender Bag

Rnd 1 (Bottom of Bag): With woodberry, ch 4, **join** *(see Pattern Notes)* in first ch to form a ring, 2 sc in

ring, [ch 4, 2 sc in ring] 5 times, do not join or turn. *(10 sc, 5 ch-4 sps)*

Rnd 2: [Ch 5, sc **in next ch-4 sp** *(see Pattern Notes)*] 5 times. *(5 sc, 5 ch-4 sps)*

Rnds 3–20: Rep rnd 3. At end of last rnd, sl st in beg sc of rnd.

Note: Work more or fewer rnds to adjust length. Any changes in length will affect yardage needed.

Rnd 21: Ch 1, sc in same st as join, 3 sc in next ch-4 sp, [sc in next st, 3 sc in next ch-4 sp] 4 times, ch 7 *(hanging lp)*, sl st in beg sc, turn. *(20 sc)*

Rnd 22: Ch 1, sc in same st as join, sc in next 7 chs, sl st in next 19 sc around. *(8 sc, 19 sl sts)*

Row 23: Sl st in next 8 sc of hanging lp, sl st in next sl st, leaving rem sts unworked. Fasten off. *(9 sl sts)*

Tassels
Make 1 in each color.

Wrap 1 strand of yarn 22 times around a 12-inch piece of cardboard. Slide an 18-inch length of yarn *(top tie)* under 1 side edge of cardboard and knot tightly over wrapped yarn to secure. Thread each end of top tie through 1 hole in button and knot tightly to secure.

Remove tassel from cardboard. Wrap an 18-inch length of yarn several times around tassel, approximately 1 inch from top tie. Tie securely and, with tapestry needle, pull ends of tie to center of Tassel.

Cut tassel ends. Thread beads on random strands as desired, knotting each bead in place at varied heights with an overhand knot.

Trim tassel ends to approximately 7 inches or as desired.

Insert button into bottom center opening of bag to attach tassel. ●

Boho Lumbar Pillow

Design by Bendy Carter

Have fun playing with stitches and color combinations in this stylish pillow design.

Skill Level

■■■□ INTERMEDIATE

Finished Measurements

9½ inches wide x 35 inches long, measured flat

Materials

- Premier Anti-Pilling Everyday Worsted medium (worsted) weight acrylic yarn (3½ oz/180 yds/100g per ball):
    - 2 balls each #100-94 pumpkin, #100-72 cloudy day, #100-07 really red and #100-78 linen
    - 1 ball each #100-19 navy and #100-28 mustard
- Size I/9/5.5mm crochet hook or size needed to obtain gauge
- Tapestry needle
- Locking stitch markers
- 12 x 36-inch pillow form
- Tassel maker *(optional)* or 5-inch piece of heavy cardboard

Gauge

12 split sc = 4 inches

Pattern Notes

To increase or decrease width of pillow cover, add or subtract multiples of 6 stitches. Enlarging pillow cover may require additional yarn.

Main color (MC) and contrasting color (CC) change in each section of Body.

Weave in ends as work progresses.

Work in continuous rounds; do not join or turn unless otherwise stated. Place stitch marker at beginning of round and move up as each round is completed.

When instructed to drop loop to change color, place stitch marker in loop to prevent unraveling. Remove marker when picking up dropped loop unless otherwise stated.

Join with slip stitch as indicated unless otherwise stated.

Special Stitches

Split single crochet in rounds (split sc): Sc in center of "V" of indicated sc.

Split Single Crochet

Single crochet join (sc join): Place a slip knot on hook, insert hook in indicated st, yo, pull up a lp, yo, draw through both lps on hook.

Front post single crochet join (fpsc join): Place a slip knot on hook, insert hook from front to back to front again around indicated st, yo, pull up a lp, yo, draw through both lps on hook.

Puff stitch (puff st): Insert hook in indicated st, yo, pull up a lp, [yo, insert hook in same st, yo, pull up a lp] twice *(6 lps on hook)*, yo, draw through all 6 lps on hook.

Note: As puff st is worked, yarn wraps around sc just made. Only top lps of sc will be visible. To find top lps easily as next rnd is worked, place st marker in lps as needed until they are recognizable.

Pillow

Foundation

Rnd 1: With pumpkin, leaving long tail for sewing, ch 61, working in **back bar of ch** *(see illustration on page 7)*, sc in 2nd ch from hook and in each ch across, being careful not to twist sts, **split sc** *(see Special Stitches)* in first st to form ring, place marker in split sc to mark as first st of next rnd. *(60 sc, 1 split sc)*

Rnd 2: Split sc in each st around to marked st, **do not join** *(see Pattern Notes)*. *(60 split sc including marked st)*

With beg tail, sew bottom of first and last st of rnd 1 tog to close rnd.

Body

Section 1: Pumpkin (MC) & navy (CC)

Rnds 1–4: With MC, split sc in each st around.

Rnd 5: Split sc in each st around to last st, sl st between legs of last st, **drop lp from hook and place on marker** *(see Pattern Notes)*. *(59 split sc, 1 sl st)*

Rnd 6: Leaving marker in first st, draw CC through marked st, sl st in next st and in each rem st around, drop lp from hook, draw MC dropped lp to back of work through marked st. *(60 sl sts)*

Rnd 7: Pick up MC lp, working above sl sts, sc in each st 2 rnds below around to last st, sl st in last st, drop lp from hook. *(59 sc, 1 sl st)*

Rnd 8: Leaving marker in first st, draw CC lp through marked st, sl st in each st around, **join** *(see Pattern Notes)* in beg sl st. Fasten off CC. *(60 sl sts)*

Rnd 9: Pick up MC dropped lp, working above sl sts, sc in each st 2 rnds below around. *(60 sc)*

Rnds 10–14: Split sc in each st around.

Rnd 15: Split sc in each st around to last st, sl st between legs of last st, join in beg sc. Fasten off. *(59 split sc, 1 sl st)*

Section 2: Cloudy day (MC) & really red (CC)

Rnd 16: Sc join *(see Special Stitches)* MC in marked st, sc in each st around, join in beg sc, drop lp from hook, draw dropped lp to back of work through beg st. *(60 sc)*

Rnd 17: Fpsc join *(see Special Stitches)* CC around first st, [ch 3, sk next 2 sts*, fpsc around next st] around, ending last rep at *, join in beg sc, drop lp from hook, draw dropped lp to back of work through beg sc. *(20 fpsc, 20 ch-3 lps)*

Rnd 18: Pick up MC dropped lp at back of work, ch 1, fpsc around first fpsc, [working behind ch-3 lp, hdc in 2 sk MC sts 2 rnds below*, fpsc around next fpsc] around, ending last rep at *, join in beg st, drop lp from hook, draw dropped lp to back of work through beg sc. *(20 fpsc, 40 hdc)*

Rnd 19: Pick up CC dropped lp at back of work, ch 1, fpsc around first fpsc, [ch 3, sk next 2 hdc*, fpsc around next fpsc] around, ending last rep at *, join in beg st, drop lp from hook, draw dropped lp to back of work through beg sc. *(20 fpsc, 20 ch-3 lps)*

Rnds 20–23: [Rep rnds 18 and 19] twice. Fasten off CC at end of last rnd.

Rnd 24: Rep rnd 18, join in beg st. Do not drop lp or draw to back of work. Fasten off. *(20 fpsc, 40 hdc)*

Section 3: Mustard (MC) & navy (CC)

Rnd 25: Sc join MC in marked st, sc in each st around. *(60 sc)*

Rnd 26: Split sc in each st around. *(60 split sc)*

Rnds 27–30: Rep rnd 26.

Rnds 31–41: Rep rnds 5–15.

Section 4: Pumpkin (MC) & linen (CC)

Rnds 42–50: Rep rnds 16–24.

Section 5: Really red (MC) & mustard (CC)

Rnd 51: Sc join MC in marked st, sc in each st around. *(60 sc)*

Rnd 52: Sc in each st around, join in beg st, drop lp from hook, draw dropped lp to back of work through beg sc. *(60 sc)*

Rnd 53: Sk marked st, sc join CC in next st, place marker in st just made as first st, [**puff st** *(see Special Stitches)* in sk st*, sk next st, sc in next st] around, ending last rep at *. Fasten off CC, leaving a long tail. Pull lp on hook until tail comes through, then draw tail to back of work through beg sc. *(30 sc, 30 puffs)*

Rnd 54: Pick up MC dropped lp at back of work, ch 1, 2 sc in marked sc, [sk puff st, 2 sc in next sc] around to last puff st, sk last puff st. *(60 sc)*

Rnd 55: Sc in each st around, join in beg sc. Fasten off MC.

Section 6: Linen (MC) & cloudy day (CC)

Rnds 56–64: Rep rnds 16–24.

Section 7: Really red (MC) & navy (CC)

Rnds 65–81: Rep rnds 25–41.

Section 8: Cloudy day (MC) & pumpkin (CC)

Rnds 82–90: Rep rnds 16–24.

Section 9: Linen (MC) & really red (CC)

Rnds 91–95: Rep rnds 51–55.

Section 10: Pumpkin (MC) & mustard (CC)

Rnds 96–104: Rep rnds 16–24.

Section 11: Cloudy day (MC) & navy (CC)

Rnds 105–121: Rep rnds 25–41.

Section 12: Pumpkin (MC) & really red (CC)

Rnds 122–130: Rep rnds 16–24.

Section 13: Linen (MC) & navy (CC)

Rnds 131–147: Rep rnds 25–41. At end of last rnd, fasten off, leaving a long tail for sewing.

Finishing

Tassel
Make 4.

Holding all 6 colors tog, follow tassel maker directions for 4-inch-long Tassel *(model shown made with 10 wraps for 120 strands)* or make as follows:

Cut 2 12-inch strands of any color and set aside.

Holding all 6 colors tog, wrap strands around 5-inch cardboard 10 times. Slide 12-inch length under 1 side edge of cardboard and knot tightly over wrapped yarn to secure. Do not trim ends of tails.

Cut across rem edge and remove cardboard. Wrap rem 12-inch length several times around Tassel, approximately 1 inch from top tie. Tie securely and, with tapestry needle, pull ends of tie to center of Tassel.

Trim bottom end of Tassel evenly to 4 inches or desired length.

Insert pillow form in cover, sew each end of cover closed. With top tails, tie Tassels to each corner. ●

Scrap Stripes Afghan

Design by Emily Carter

This bright and fun afghan is a quick stitch! You can also use yarn scraps, making this project a great stash buster!

Skill Level

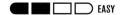 EASY

Finished Measurements

45 inches wide x 59 inches long

Materials

- Red Heart Super Saver medium (worsted) weight acrylic yarn (7 oz/364 yds/198g per skein):
  - 1 skein each #235 lemon, #506 pool, #347 light periwinkle, #320 cornmeal, #776 dark orchid and #259 flamingo
  - 2 skeins #718 shocking pink
- Size H/8/5mm crochet hook or size needed to obtain gauge
- Tapestry needle

Gauge

8 dc rows = 4 inches; 11 dc sts = 4 inches

Pattern Notes

Chain-2 at beginning of row does not count as first double crochet unless otherwise stated.

Color sequence is a 56-stripe pattern worked twice for afghan.

Join with slip stitch as indicated unless otherwise stated.

Color Sequence

6 rows shocking pink, 2 rows flamingo, 3 rows lemon, 1 row pool, 3 rows lemon, 2 rows flamingo, 6 rows shocking pink, 4 rows cornmeal, 1 row dark orchid, 4 rows cornmeal, 5 rows flamingo, 1 row lemon, 2 rows light periwinkle, 3 rows pool, 1 row cornmeal, 1 row pool, 3 rows dark orchid, 1 row pool, 1 row cornmeal, 3 rows pool, 2 rows light periwinkle and 1 row lemon.

Afghan

Row 1: With shocking pink, ch 127, dc in 3rd ch from hook, dc in each rem ch across, turn. *(125 dc)*

Row 2: Ch 2 *(see Pattern Notes)*, dc in each dc across, turn. *(125 dc)*

Rows 3–112: Rep row 2, working Color Sequence. Leaving a 2-inch length, fasten off at end of each color sequence.

Border

Rnd 1: Join *(see Pattern Notes)* shocking pink in any dc on row 112 away from corner, ch 1, hdc evenly sp around outer edge of afghan, working (hdc, ch 1, hdc) in each corner, join in beg hdc. Fasten off. ●

Boho Chic Storage Basket

Design by Brenda Bourg

Granny squares and stripes come together to create this
cute little basket that will tidy up your space.

Skill Level

 EASY

Finished Measurements

7 inches wide x 7 inches deep x 7½ inches tall

Materials

- Premier Cotton Fair Bulky bulky
  (chunky) weight cotton/acrylic
  yarn (3½ oz/153 yds/100g per ball):
    - 3 balls #2081-12 cornflower (A)
    - 2 balls #2081-13 cadet (B)
    - 1 ball each #2081-14 turquoise (C),
      #2081-15 leap frog (D), #2081-07 red (E),
      #2081-03 daffodil (F), #2081-10 violet (G),
      #2081-20 sand (H), #2081-06 bubblegum
      (J) and #2081-04 peach (K)
- Size K/10½/6.5mm crochet hook or size
  needed to obtain gauge
- Tapestry needle
- Heavy cardboard or stiff plastic canvas
  (optional)

Gauge

10 hdc = 4 inches; 7 hdc rows = 4 inches

Pattern Notes

Basket is designed to be filled and will stand up
after items are added. If Basket is intended to stand
upright without contents, line with optional heavy
cardboard or stiff plastic canvas.

Begin and end each color with extra-long tails. For
added thickness and stability, weave in ends back
and forth through fabric as work progresses.

Join with slip stitch as indicated unless
otherwise stated.

Motifs and Squares are worked with right side facing
at all times. Do not turn work unless otherwise stated.

Chain-2 at beginning of row counts as first half
double crochet unless otherwise stated.

Special Stitches

Beginning cluster (beg cl): Ch 3, [yo, insert hook in same sp, yo, pull lp through, yo, pull through 2 lps on hook] 2 times, yo, pull through all 3 lps on hook.

Cluster (cl): Yo, insert hook in next sp, yo, pull lp through, yo, pull through 2 lps on hook, [yo, insert hook in same sp, yo, pull lp through, yo, pull through 2 lps on hook] 2 times, yo, pull through all lps on hook.

Single crochet join (sc join): Place a slip knot on hook, insert hook in indicated st, yo, pull up a lp, yo and draw through both lps on hook.

Double crochet join (dc join): Place slip knot on hook, yo, insert hook in indicated st, yo, pull up a lp *(3 lps on hook)*, [yo, draw through 2 lps] twice.

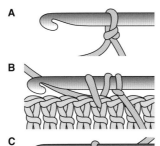

Double Crochet Join

Basket

Motif 1

Rnd 1: With J and leaving a **long tail** *(see Pattern Notes)*, ch 5, **join** *(see Pattern Notes)* in first ch to form ring, **beg cl** *(see Special Stitches)*, ch 2, [cl *(see Special Stitches)* in ring, ch 2] 7 times, join in top of beg cl. Fasten off. *(8 ch-2 sps)*

Rnd 2: With RS facing *(see Pattern Notes)*, **sc join** *(see Special Stitches)* D in any ch-2 sp, 3 sc in same sp, 4 sc in each ch-2 sp around, join in beg sc. Fasten off. *(32 sc)*

Rnd 3: Sc join G in any st, ch 5, sc in same st, [ch 3, sk next 2 sts, sc in next st, ch 3, sk next st, sc in next st, ch 3, sk next 2 sts*, (sc, ch 5, sc) in next st] around, ending last rep at *, join in beg sc. Fasten off. *(16 sc, 4 ch-1 sps, 8 ch-3 sps, 4 ch-5 corner sps)*

Rnd 4: Sc join B in any ch-5 corner sp, 2 sc in same sp, [2 sc in next 3 ch-3 sps*, 3 sc in next ch-5 corner sp] around, ending last rep at *, join in beg sc. Fasten off. *(4 3-sc corners, 24 sc)*

Rnd 5: Dc join *(see Special Stitches)* E in center st of any 3-sc corner, 2 dc in same st, [dc in each st around to center st of next 3-sc corner*, 3 dc in center st] around, ending last rep at *, join in beg dc. Fasten off. *(4 3-dc corners, 32 dc)*

Rnd 6: Sc join A in any dc, sc in each st around, working 3 sc in center st of each 3-dc corner, join in top of ch-3. Fasten off. *(4 3-sc corners, 44 sc)*

Motif 2

Note: Work all rnds same as Motif 1 with indicated color.

Rnd 1: G.	**Rnd 2:** K.
Rnd 3: H.	**Rnd 4:** F.
Rnd 5: B.	**Rnd 6:** A.

Bottom Square

Row 1: With G, ch 15, hdc in 2nd ch from hook and in each ch across. Fasten off. *(14 hdc)*

Row 2: With RS facing, join H in beg hdc, **ch 2** *(see Pattern Notes)*, hdc in each st across. Fasten off.

Note: In rows 3–10, rep row 2 with indicated color.

Row 3: C.	**Row 4:** K.
Row 5: J.	**Row 6:** E.
Row 7: D.	**Row 8:** B.
Row 9: F.	**Row 10:** H.

Border

Rnd 1: Sc join A in first hdc of last row, 2 sc in same st, sc in each st across to last st, 3 sc in last sc, *working in ends of rows, sc evenly across side edge*, working in opposite side of foundation ch, 3 sc in first ch, sc in each ch across to last ch, 3 sc in last ch, rep between *, join in beg sc. Fasten off. *(4 3-sc corners)*

Rnd 2: Working in **back lps** *(see StitchGuide.com)*, sc join B in center st of any corner, 2 sc in same st, sc in each st around, working 3 sc in center st of each corner, join in beg sc. Fasten off.

Rnd 3: With A, rep rnd 2.

Side Square 1
Note: Work rows same as Bottom Square with indicated color.

Row 1: D.	**Row 2:** K.
Row 3: E.	**Row 4:** F.
Row 5: B.	**Row 6:** H.
Row 7: H.	**Row 8:** C.
Row 9: G.	**Row 10:** F.

Border
With A, work same as rnd 1 of Bottom Square Border.

Side Square 2
Note: Work rows same as Bottom Square with indicated color.

Row 1: E.	**Row 2:** B.
Row 3: H.	**Row 4:** C.
Row 5: K.	**Row 6:** G.
Row 7: D.	**Row 8:** F.
Row 9: J.	**Row 10:** B.

Border
With A, work same as rnd 1 of Bottom Square Border.

Handle
Make 2.

With E and leaving a long tail for sewing, ch 30, sl st in 2nd ch from hook and each ch across. Fasten off, leaving a long tail for sewing.

Finishing
Block each piece to 7-inch square.

Rotate Side Square 2 so rows are vertical. Alternating designs and working through back lps of side edges, sew Motifs and Side Squares tog.

Working through back lps, sew Bottom Square to lower edges of Motifs and Squares.

Top Edge
Rnd 1: Working in back lps, sc join B in any st, sc in each st around, join in beg sc. Fasten off.

Rnd 2: With A, rep rnd 1.

Handles
With beg and end tails and referring to photo as a guide, sew Handles to each Side Square. ●

Aegean Towel Holder

Design by Britt Schmiesing

Hook these towel rings over your oven door handle or bar and insert any kitchen towel you choose through the rings.

Skill Level

 BEGINNER

Finished Measurements

3 inches wide x 9½ inches long, excluding rings

Materials

- Premier Yarns Home Cotton medium (worsted) weight cotton/ polyester yarn (2½ oz/131 yds/75g per skein):
    1 skein each #38-01 white, #38-39 driftwood and #38-13 pastel blue
- Size H/8/5mm crochet hook or size needed to obtain gauge
- 3-inch-diameter wood rings: 2 per towel holder
- Tapestry needle

Scan code for a video on how to crochet over a ring.

Gauge

11 hdc = 3 inches

Gauge isn't critical for this project.

Pattern Notes

One skein can make a few of these ringed towel holders.

Use extra-long starting and ending tails to attach towel holder to rings. Or scan the code to see how to work your crochet directly around the rings.

Towel Holder

Make 1 in each color.

Row 1: Leaving a 2-yd starting tail *(see Pattern Notes)*, ch 12, hdc in 3rd ch from hook *(sk chs count as first hdc)* and each rem ch across, turn. *(11 hdc)*

Row 2: Ch 1 *(doesn't count as a st)*, hdc in first and each st across, turn.

Rep row 2 until holder measures 9½ inches from start. Fasten off, leaving a 2-yd tail.

Finishing

Hold 1 short end of towel holder beside ring. Thread yarn tail on tapestry needle. *Bring tail up through ring and down through first st on short end twice, rep from * across short end, fasten off and weave in end.

Rep on opposite short end. ●

Terra-Cotta Skies Centerpiece

Design by Mary Beth Temple

Beautiful colors and an elegant design
featuring picots and shells come together
to create a one-of-a-kind centerpiece.

Skill Level

■■□□ EASY

Finished Measurement
27 inches in diameter from largest point to largest
point, blocked

Materials

- Premier Anti-Pilling Everyday Worsted medium (worsted) weight acrylic yarn (1¾ oz/90 yds/50g per skein):
  - 1 skein each indigo (A), cerulean (B), cream (C), rococo rose (D) and peach sand (E)
- Size I/9/5.5mm crochet hook or size needed to obtain gauge
- Tapestry needle

Gauge

Rnds 1–4: 4 inches from point to point after blocking

Pattern Notes

Weave in loose ends as work progresses.

Join with slip stitch as indicated unless otherwise stated.

Chain-2 at beginning of round counts as first half double crochet otherwise stated.

Chain-3 at beginning of round counts as first double crochet otherwise stated.

Chain-4 at beginning of round counts as first treble crochet unless otherwise stated.

Special Stitches

Picot: Ch 3, sl st in 3rd ch from hook.

Picot shell: (Hdc, dc, tr, **picot**—*see Special Stitches*, dc, hdc) in indicated st.

Centerpiece

Rnd 1 (RS): With A, make **slip ring** (*see illustration on page 12*), ch 1, 6 sc in ring, **join** (*see Pattern Notes*) in first sc, pull end to close ring. *(6 sc)*

Rnd 2: Ch 3 (*see Pattern Notes*), dc in same sc, ch 1, [2 dc in next sc, ch 1] 5 times, join rnd in 3rd ch of beg ch-3. *(12 dc, 6 ch-1 sps)*

Rnd 3: Ch 1, sc in same dc, sc in next dc, 2 sc in next ch-1 sp, [sc in next 2 dc, 2 sc in next ch-1 sp] 5 times,

change color (*see StitchGuide.com*) to B in last st, join rnd in first sc. Fasten off A. *(24 sc)*

Rnd 4: With B, ch 1, sc in same st, sk next sc, 5 dc in next sc, [sk next sc, sc in next sc, sk next sc, 5 dc in next sc] 5 times, changing to C in last st, join in first sc. Fasten off B. *(6 5-dc groups, 6 sc)*

Rnd 5: With C, ch 3, 3 dc in same sc, sk next 2 dc, sc in next dc, [sk next 2 dc, 7 dc in next sc, sk next 2 dc, sc in next dc] 5 times, sk next 2 dc, 3 dc in first sc, changing to D in last st, join in 3rd ch of beg ch-3. Fasten off C. *(6 7-dc groups, 6 sc)*

Rnd 6: With D, ch 1, sc in same st, sk next 3 dc, ([tr, ch 1] 4 times) in next sc, tr in same sc, [sk next 3 dc, sc in next dc, sk next 3 dc, ({tr, ch 1} 4 times) in next sc, tr in same sc] 5 times, changing to E in last st, join rnd in first sc. Fasten off D. *(30 tr, 24 ch-1 sps, 6 sc)*

Rnd 7: With E, ch 1, sc in same sc, *ch 1, hdc in next tr, ch 1, dc in next tr, ch 1, (tr, ch 1, tr, ch 1, tr) in next tr, ch 1, dc in next tr, ch 1, hdc in next tr, ch 1**, sc in next sc, rep from * 5 times, ending last rep at **, changing to D in last st, join in first sc. Fasten off E. *(18 tr, 12 dc, 12, hdc, 6 sc, 42 ch-1 sps)*

Rnd 8: With D, ch 1, sc in same sc, *ch 1, hdc in next hdc, ch 1, dc in next dc, ch 1, dc in next tr, ch 1, (tr, ch 2, tr, ch 2, tr) in next tr, ch 1, dc in next tr, ch 1, dc in next dc, ch 1, hdc in next hdc, ch 1**, sc in next sc, rep from * 5 times, ending last rep at **, changing to C in last st, join in first sc. Fasten off D. *(18 tr, 24 dc, 12 hdc, 6 sc, 48 ch-1 sps, 12 ch-2 sps)*

Rnd 9: With C, ch 3, 2 dc in same sc, *sk next 2 ch-1 sps, sc in next dc, [sc in next ch-1 sp, sc in next st] twice, 2 sc in next ch-2 sp, 3 sc in next tr, 2 sc in next ch-2 sp, sc in next tr, [sc in next ch-1 sp, sc in next st] twice, sk next 2 ch-1 sps**, 5 dc in next sc, rep from * 5 times, ending last rep at **, 2 dc in first sc, changing to B in last st, join in top of beg ch-3. Fasten off C. *(6 5-dc groups, 102 sc)*

Rnd 10: With B, ch 1, sc in same st, *sk next 2 dc, 2 hdc in next sc, sk next 2 sc, sc in next 5 sc, 3 sc in next sc, sc in next 5 sc, sk next 2 sc, 2 hdc in next sc, sk next 2 dc**, sc in next dc, rep from * 5 times, ending last rep at **, changing to A in last st, join in first sc. Fasten off B. *(24 hdc, 84 sc)*

Rnd 11: With A, **ch 4** *(see Pattern Notes)*, tr in same sc, *tr in next hdc, dc in next 2 sts, hdc in next 2 sts, sc in next 7 sts, hdc in next 2 sts, dc in next 2 sts, tr in next hdc**, 3 tr in next sc, rep from * 5 times, ending last rep at **, tr in first sc, changing to B in last st, join in top of beg ch-4. Fasten off A. *(30 tr, 24 dc, 24 hdc, 42 sc)*

Rnd 12: With B, ch 4, tr in same st, *tr in next 5 sts, dc in next 2 sts, hdc in next sc, sc in next 3 sts, hdc in next sc, dc in next 2 sts, tr in next 5 sts**, 3 tr in next tr, rep from * 5 times, ending last rep at **, tr in first tr, changing to C in last st, join rnd in top of beg ch-4. Fasten off B. *(78 tr, 24 dc, 12 hdc, 18 sc)*

Rnd 13: With C, ch 1, **sc dec** *(see StitchGuide.com)* in first 2 sts, sc in next 53 sts, sc dec in next 2 sc, sc in each rem st around, join in first sc. *(130 sc)*

Rnd 14: Ch 1, sc in same sc, sk next sc, 5 dc in next sc, sk next 2 sc, *sc in next sc, sk next sc, 5 dc in next sc, sk next 2 sc, rep from * around, changing to D in last st, join in first sc. Fasten off C. *(26 5-dc groups, 26 sc)*

Rnd 15: With D, ch 3, 2 dc in same sc, sk next 2 dc, sc in next dc, sk next 2 dc, 7 dc in next sc, sk next 2 dc, sc in next dc, sk next 2 dc, *5 dc in next sc, sk next 2 dc, sc in next dc, sk next 2 dc, 7 dc in next sc, sk next 2 dc, sc in next dc, sk next 2 dc, rep from * around, 2 dc in first sc, changing to E in last st, join in top of beg ch-3. Fasten off D. *(13 7-dc groups, 13 5-dc groups, 26 sc)*

Rnd 16: With E, ch 1, sc in same st, sk next 2 dc, 7 dc in next sc, sk next 3 dc, sc in next dc, sk next 3 dc, 7 dc in next sc, sk next 2 dc, *sc in next dc, sk next 2 dc, 7 dc in next sc, sk next 3 dc, sc in next dc, sk next 3 dc, 7 dc in next sc, sk next 2 dc, rep from * around, changing to D in last st, join in first sc. Fasten off E. *(26 7-dc groups, 26 sc)*

Rnd 17: With D, ch 4, 3 tr in same sc, sk next 3 dc, sc in next dc, sk next 3 dc, 9 **dtr** *(see StitchGuide.com)* in next sc, sk next 3 dc, sc in next dc, sk next 3 dc, *7 tr in next sc, sk next 3 dc, sc in next dc, sk next 3 dc, 9 dtr in next sc, sk next 3 dc, sc in next dc, rep from * around, sk next 3 dc, 3 tr in first sc, changing to C in last st, join in top of beg ch-4. Fasten off D. *(13 9-dtr groups, 13 7-tr groups, 26 sc)*

Rnd 18: Ch 1, 2 sc in same st, sc in next 2 sts, sc dec in next 3 sts, sc in next 3 sts, 3 sc in next st, sc in next 3 sts, sc dec in next 3 sts, *sc in next 2 sts, 3 sc in next st, sc in next 2 sts, sc dec in next 3 sts, sc in next 3 sts, 3 sc in next st, sc in next 3 sts, sc dec in next 3 sts, rep from * 11 times, sc in next 2 sts, sc in first st, changing to B in last st, join in first sc. Fasten off C. *(234 sc)*

Rnd 19: With B, **ch 2** *(see Pattern Notes)*, 2 hdc in same st, sc in next 2 sc, sc dec in next 3 sc, sc in next 3 sc, 5 hdc in next sc, sc in next 3 sc, sc dec in next 3 sc, *sc in next 2 sc, 5 hdc in next sc, sc in next 2 sc, sc dec in next 3 sc, sc in next 3 sc, 5 hdc in next sc, sc in next 3 sc, sc dec in next 3 sc, rep from * 11 times, sc in next 2 sc, 2 hdc in first st, changing to A in last st, join in top of beg ch-2. Fasten off B. *(26 5-hdc groups, 156 sc)*

Rnd 20: With A, ch 2, 2 hdc in same st, sc in next 3 sts, sc dec in next 3 sc, sc in next 4 sts, **picot shell**—*see Special Stitches* in next hdc, sc in next 4 sts, sc dec in next 3 sc, *sc in next 3 sts, 5 hdc in next hdc, sc in next 3 sts, sc dec in next 3 sc, sc in next 4 sts, picot shell in next hdc, sc in next 4 sts, sc dec in next 3 sc, rep from * 11 times, sc in next 3 sc, 3 hdc in first st, join in top of beg ch-2. Fasten off. *(182 sc, 13 picot shells, 13 5-hdc groups, 208 sc)*

Finishing
Block to finished measurements. ●

Moroccan Tile Coasters

Designs by Lena Skvagerson

Create these beautifully stitched coasters in no time to add just a touch of Mediterranean style to any tabletop.

Skill Level
 INTERMEDIATE

Finished Measurement
7¼ inches

Materials
- Premier Anti-Pilling Everyday Worsted medium (worsted) weight acrylic yarn (1¾ oz/90 yds/ 50g per skein):
  - 2 skeins indigo
  - 1 skein each cream, rococo rose and peach sand
  - Scraps cerulean and spice
- Size I/9/5.5mm crochet hook or size needed to obtain gauge
- Tapestry needle

Gauge
12 sc = 4 inches; 15 sc rows = 4 inches

To save time, take time to check gauge.

Pattern Notes
Join with slip stitch as indicated unless otherwise stated.

Scan code to see a video about how to work a split fptr cl, also called fptr2tog.

Weave in loose ends as work progresses.

Chain-1 at beginning of round does not count as a stitch unless otherwise stated.

Chain-2 at beginning of round counts as first half double crochet unless otherwise stated.

Chain-3 at beginning of round counts as first double crochet unless otherwise stated.

When changing color at end of round, change to new color by drawing loop of new color through joining stitch and loop on hook.

Special Stitch
Split front post treble crochet cluster (split fptr cl): *Yo twice, insert hook around post of indicated st, [yo, draw through 2 lps on hook] twice, rep from * once, yo, draw through all lps on hook.

Coasters

Coaster 1
Make 3.

Rnd 1: With cerulean, ch 2, 6 sc in first ch, **join** *(see Pattern Notes)* in first sc to form ring. *(6 sc)*

Rnd 2: Ch 2 *(see Pattern Notes)*, hdc in same st as ch, 2 hdc in each sc around, **changing color** *(see Pattern Notes)* to indigo, join in top of beg ch-2. *(12 hdc)* Fasten off cerulean.

Rnd 3: Ch 3 *(see Pattern Notes)*, dc in same st as ch, working in **back bar** *(see illustration)* of each hdc, work [2 dc in next hdc] around, join in top of beg ch-3. *(24 dc)*

Half Double Crochet Back Bar Working in Rounds (illustration shows side facing away from stitcher)

Coaster 1

Coaster 2

Rnd 4: Ch 2, hdc in next dc, 2 hdc in next dc, [hdc in next 2 dc, 2 hdc in next dc] around, changing to cream, join in top of beg ch-2. *(32 hdc)*

Rnd 5: Ch 1 *(see Pattern Notes)*, sc in same st as ch, working in back bar of each hdc around, in next corner hdc work (2 sc, ch 2, 2 sc), sc in next hdc, **split fptr cl** *(see Special Stitch)* with first leg around post of ch-3 at beg of rnd 2 rnds below, sk 2 dc 2 rnds below, work 2nd leg around post of next dc 2 rnds below, sk next hdc on current rnd, [sc in next 3 hdc, split fptr cl with first leg around post of same dc as last fptr worked, sk 2 dc 2 rnds below, work 2nd leg around post of next dc 2 rnds below, sk next hdc on current rnd, sc in next hdc, in next corner hdc work (2 sc, ch 2, 2 sc), sc in next hdc, split fptr cl with first leg around post of same dc as last fptr worked, sk 2 dc 2 rnds below, work 2nd leg around post of next dc 2 rnds below, sk next hdc on current rnd] 3 times, sc in next 3 hdc, split fptr cl with first leg around post of same dc as last fptr worked, sk 2 dc 2 rnds below, work 2nd leg around same ch-3 post 2 rnds below as beg tr, sk next hdc on current rnd, changing to indigo, join in beg sc. *(44 sts; 11 sts along each side, ch-2 sp in each corner)* Fasten off cream.

Rnd 6: Ch 2, hdc in next 2 sc, [3 hdc in corner ch-2 sp, hdc in next 11 sts] 3 times, 3 hdc in last corner ch-2 sp, hdc in last 8 sts, changing to peach sand, join in top of beg ch-2. *(56 hdc; 13 hdc along each side, 1 hdc in each corner)*

Rnd 7: Ch 1, sc in same st, working in back bar of each hdc around, work sc in next 3 hdc, [3 sc in corner hdc, sc in next 13 hdc] 3 times, 3 sc in last corner hdc, sc in last 9 hdc, changing to indigo, join in **back lp** *(see StitchGuide.com)* at top of beg sc. *(64 sc; 15 sc along each side, 1 sc in each corner)*

Rnd 8: Ch 1, sc in back lp of same st, working in back lp of each st around, work sc in next 4 sc, [3 sc in corner sc, sc in next 5 sc, reaching in front of sc on previous rnd, work dc in back lp of next 5 hdc 2 rnds below, sc in next 5 sc on previous rnd] 3 times, 3 sc in last corner sc, sc in next 5 sc, reaching in front of sc on previous rnd, work dc in back lp of next 5 hdc 2 rnds below, changing to peach sand, join in back lp of beg sc. *(72 sts; 17 sts along each side, 1 sc in each corner)*

Rnd 9: Ch 1, reaching in front of first sc on previous rnd, work dc in **front lp** *(see StitchGuide.com)* of same st 2 rnds below, working in back lp of each st around, work sc in next 5 sc, [3 sc in corner sc, sc in next 5 sc, {reaching in front of next sc on previous rnd, work dc in front lp of sc 2 rnds below, sc in next 5 sts on previous rnd} twice] 3 times, 3 sc in last corner sc, sc in next 5 sc, reaching in front of next sc on previous rnd, work dc in front lp of sc 2 rnds below, sc in next 5 sts on previous rnd, changing to indigo, join in back lp of beg dc. *(80 sts; 19 sts along each side, 1 sc in each corner)* Fasten off peach sand.

Rnd 10: Ch 1, sc in back lp of same st, reaching in front of next sc on previous rnd, work dc in front lp of same st 2 rnds below, working in back lp of each st around, work sc in next 5 sc, [3 sc in corner sc, sc in next 5 sc, {reaching in front of next sc on previous rnd, work dc in front lp of sc 2 rnds below, sc in next 3 sts on previous rnd} twice, reaching in front of next sc on previous rnd, work dc in front lp of st 2 rnds below, sc in next 5 sc on previous rnd] 3 times, 3 sc in corner sc, sc in next 5 sc, reaching in front of next sc on previous rnd, work dc in front lp of sc 2 rnds below, sc in next 3 sts on previous rnd, reaching in front of next sc on previous rnd, work dc in front lp of dc 2 rnds below, sc in last 2 sc on previous rnd, changing to spice, join in back lp of beg sc. *(88 sts; 21 sts along each side, 1 sc in each corner)*

Rnd 11: Ch 1, sc in back lp of same st, sc in back lp of next st, reaching in front of next sc on previous rnd, work dc in front lp of same st 2 rnds below, working in back lp of each st around, work sc in next 5 sc, [3 sc in corner sc, sc in next 5 sc, reaching in front of next sc on previous rnd, work dc in front lp of sc 2 rnds below, sc in next 3 sts on previous rnd, reaching in front of next sc on previous rnd, work dc in front lp of sc 2 rnds below, sc in next st on previous rnd, reaching in front of next sc on previous rnd, work dc in front lp of sc 2 rnds below, sc in next 3 sts on previous rnd, reaching in front of next sc on previous rnd, work dc in front lp of sc 2 rnds below, sc in next 5 sts on previous rnd] 3 times, 3 sc in corner sc, sc in next 5 sc, reaching in front of next sc on previous rnd, work dc in front lp of sc 2 rnds below, sc in next 3 sts on previous rnd, reaching in front of next sc on previous rnd, work dc in front lp of sc 2 rnds below, sc in next st on previous rnd, reaching in front of next sc on previous rnd, work dc in front lp of sc 2 rnds below, sc in last sc on previous rnd, changing to indigo, join in back lp of beg sc. *(96 sts; 23 sts along each side, 1 sc in each corner)* Fasten off spice.

Rnd 12: Ch 1, sc in back lp of same st, working in back lp of each st around, sc in next 8 sts, [sc in corner sc, sc in next 11 sts, reaching in front of next sc on previous rnd, work dc in front lp of dc 2 rnds below, sc in next 11 sts on previous rnd] 3 times, sc in corner sc, sc in next 11 sts, reaching in front of next sc on previous rnd, work dc in front lp of dc 2 rnds below, sc in last 2 sts on previous rnd, join in beg sc. Fasten off. *(96 sts; 23 sts along each side, 1 sc in each corner)*

Coaster 2
Make 3.

Rnd 1: With cream, ch 2, 8 sc in first ch, **changing color** *(see Pattern Notes)* to cerulean, **join** *(see Pattern Notes)* in first sc to form ring. *(8 sc)* Fasten off cream.

Rnd 2: Ch 1 *(see Pattern Notes)*, in same st work (sc, ch 2, sc), [sc in next sc, in next sc work (sc, ch 2, sc)] 3 times, sc in last sc, changing to indigo, join in **back lp** *(see StitchGuide.com)* of beg sc. *(20 sts; 3 sc along each side, 2 chs in each corner)*

Rnd 3: Ch 1, sc in back lp of same st, working in back lp of each sc around, [in corner ch sp work (sc, ch 2, sc), sc in next 3 sc] 3 times, in last corner ch sp work (sc, ch 2, sc), sc in next 2 sc, join in back lp of beg sc. *(28 sts; 5 sc along each side, 2 chs in each corner)*

Rnd 4: Ch 1, sc in back lp of same st, working in back lp of each sc around, sc in next sc, [in corner

ch sp work (sc, ch 2, sc), sc in next 5 sc] 3 times, in last corner ch sp work (sc, ch 2, sc), sc in next 3 sc, changing to cerulean, join in back lp of beg sc. *(36 sts; 7 sc along each side, 2 chs in each corner)*

Rnd 5: Ch 1, tr in **front lp** *(see StitchGuide.com)* of st 2 rnds below same st as ch, [sc in back lp of next 2 sc, in corner ch sp work (sc, ch 2, sc), sc in back lp of next 2 sc, {tr in front lp of st 2 rnds below next st} 3 times] 3 times, sc in back lp of next 2 sc, in last corner ch sp work (sc, ch 2, sc), sc in back lp of next 2 sc, [tr in front lp of st 2 rnds below next st] twice, join in beg tr. *(44 sts; 9 sts along each side, 2 chs in each corner)*

Rnd 6: Ch 1, sc in same st as ch, sc in back lp of next 3 sc, [in corner ch sp work (sc, ch 2, sc), sc in back lp of next 3 sc, sc in both lps of next 3 tr, sc in back lp of next 3 sc] 3 times, in last corner ch sp work (sc, ch 2, sc), sc in back lp of next 3 sc, sc in both lps of next 2 tr, join in beg sc, sl st in next sc, changing to indigo, sl st in next sc. *(44 sts; 11 sts along each side, ch-2 sp in each corner)* Fasten off cerulean.

Rnd 7: Ch 1, dc in front lp of st 1 rnd below same st as ch, dc in front lp of st 1 rnd below next st, hdc in next sc, [3 hdc in corner ch-2 sp, hdc in next sc, {dc in front lp of st 1 rnd below next st} 3 times, hdc in next 3 sc, {dc in front lp of st 1 rnd below next st} 3 times, hdc in next sc] 3 times, 3 hdc in last corner ch-2 sp, hdc in next sc, {dc in front lp of st 1 rnd below next st} 3 times, hdc in next 3 sc, dc in front lp of st 1 rnd below next st, changing to rococo rose, join in beg dc. *(56 sts; 13 sts along each side, 1 hdc in each corner)*

Rnd 8: Ch 1, sc in same st, working in back bar of each st around, work sc in next 3 sts, [3 sc in corner hdc, sc in next 13 sts] 3 times, 3 sc in last corner hdc, sc in last 9 sts, changing to indigo, join in back lp of beg sc. *(64 sc; 15 sc along each side, 1 sc in each corner)*

Rnd 9: Ch 1, sc in back lp of same st, working in back lp of each st around, work sc in next 4 sc, [3 sc in corner sc, sc in next 5 sc, reaching in front of sc on previous rnd, work dc in back lp of next 5 sts 2 rnds below, sc in next 5 sc on previous rnd] 3 times, 3 sc in last corner sc, sc in next 5 sc, reaching in front of sc on previous rnd, work dc in back lp of next 5 sts 2 rnds below, changing to rococo rose, join in back lp of beg sc. *(72 sts; 17 sts along each side, 1 sc in each corner)*

Rnd 10: Ch 1, reaching in front of first sc on previous rnd, work dc in front lp of same st 2 rnds below, working in back lp of each st around, work sc in next 5 sc, [3 sc in corner sc, sc in next 5 sc, {reaching in front of next sc on previous rnd, work dc in front lp of sc 2 rnds below, sc in next 5 sts on previous rnd} twice] 3 times, 3 sc in last corner sc, sc in next 5 sc, reaching in front of next sc on previous rnd, work dc in front lp of sc 2 rnds below, sc in next 5 sts on previous rnd, changing to indigo, join in back lp of beg dc. *(80 sts; 19 sts along each side, 1 sc in each corner)* Fasten off rococo rose.

Rnd 11: Ch 1, sc in back lp of same st, reaching in front of next sc on previous rnd, work dc in front lp of same st 2 rnds below, working in back lp of each st around, work sc in next 5 sc, [3 sc in corner sc, sc in next 5 sc, {reaching in front of next sc on previous rnd, work dc in front lp of sc 2 rnds below, sc in next 3 sts on previous rnd} twice, reaching in front of next sc on previous rnd, work dc in front lp of st 2 rnds below, sc in next 5 sc on previous rnd] 3 times, 3 sc in corner sc, sc in next 5 sc, reaching in front of next sc on previous rnd, work dc in front lp of sc 2 rnds below, sc in next 3 sts on previous rnd, reaching in front of next sc on previous rnd, work dc in front lp of dc 2 rnds below, sc in last 2 sc on previous rnd, changing to peach sand, join in back lp of beg sc. *(88 sts; 21 sts along each side, 1 sc in each corner)*

Rnd 12: Ch 1, sc in back lp of same st, sc in back lp of next st, reaching in front of next sc on previous rnd, work dc in front lp of same st 2 rnds below, working in back lp of each st around, work sc in next 5 sc, [3 sc in corner sc, sc in next 5 sc, reaching in front of next sc on previous rnd, work dc in front lp of sc 2 rnds below, sc in next 3 sts on previous rnd, reaching in front of next sc on previous rnd, work dc in front lp of sc 2 rnds below, sc in next st on previous rnd, reaching in front of next sc on previous rnd, work dc in front lp of sc 2 rnds below, sc in next 3 sts on previous rnd, reaching in front of next sc on previous rnd, work dc in front lp of sc 2 rnds below, sc in next 5 sts on previous rnd] 3 times, 3 sc in corner sc, sc in next 5 sc, reaching in front of next sc on previous rnd, work dc in front lp of sc 2 rnds below, sc in next 3 sts on previous rnd, reaching in front of next sc on previous rnd, work dc in front lp of sc 2 rnds below, sc in next st on previous rnd, reaching in front of next sc on previous rnd, work dc in front lp of sc 2 rnds below, sc in last sc on previous rnd, changing to indigo, join in back lp of beg sc. *(96 sts; 23 sts along each side, 1 sc in each corner)* Fasten off peach sand.

Rnd 13: Ch 1, sc in back lp of same st, working in back lp of each st around, sc in next 8 sts, [sc in corner sc, sc in next 11 sts, reaching in front of next sc on previous rnd, work dc in front lp of dc 2 rnds below, sc in next 11 sts on previous rnd] 3 times, sc in corner sc, sc in next 11 sts, reaching in front of next sc on previous rnd, work dc in front lp of dc 2 rnds below, sc in last 2 sts on previous rnd, join in beg sc. *(96 sts; 23 sts along each side, 1 sc each corner)* Fasten off.

Finishing
Weave in all ends. ●

Ionian
Hexagon Tile Throw

Design by Jennifer Olivarez

Hexagon and half-hexagon motifs using a variety of
stitches combine to create this blanket inspired by
the colors of the Mediterranean Ionian Islands.

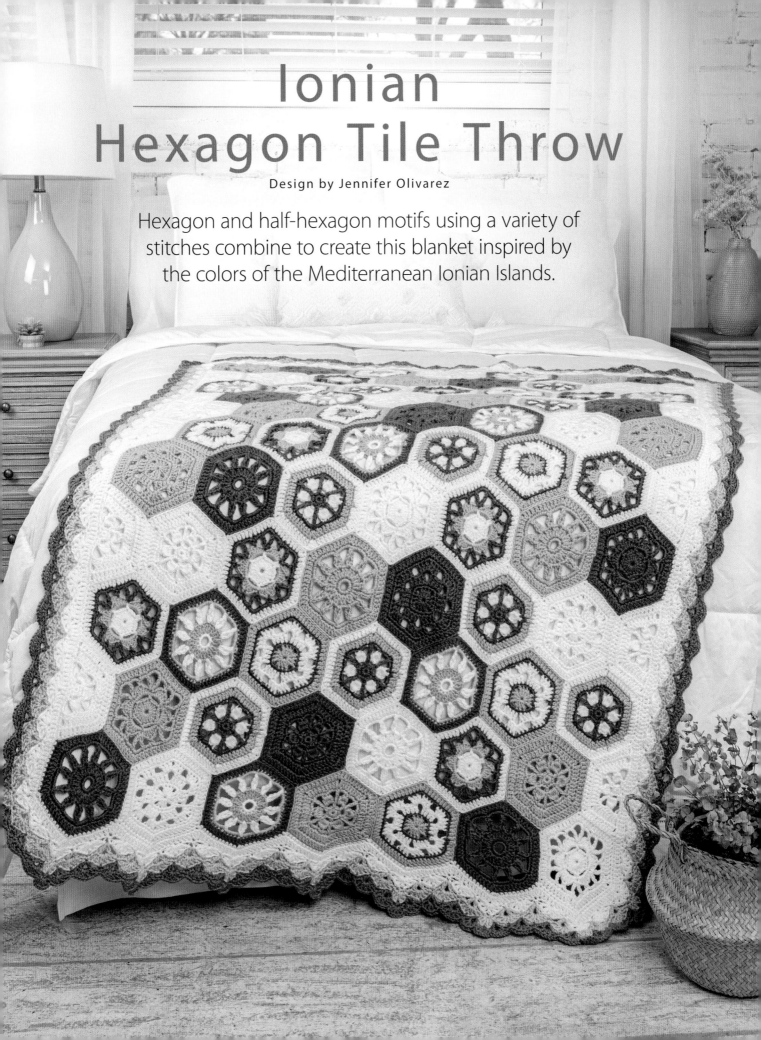

Skill Level

 INTERMEDIATE

Finished Measurements

41 inches wide x 53 inches long

Materials

- Premier Yarns Anti-Pilling Worsted medium (worsted) weight acrylic yarn (3½ oz/180 yds/100g per skein):
  - 5 skeins #100-01 snow white (A)
  - 3 skeins each #100-48 quiet blue (B) and #100-47 twilight blue (C)
  - 1 skein each #100-51 spa (D) and #100-91 lake (E)
- Size H/8/5mm crochet hook or size needed to obtain gauge
- Stitch markers: 4
- Tapestry needle

Gauge

Hexagon Motifs: 5½ inches at widest point

Pattern Notes

Motifs are joined into 11 strips, and then strips are joined together. A 3-inch border is added after seaming.

Join with slip stitch as indicated unless otherwise stated.

Chain-3 at beginning of round or row counts as first double crochet unless otherwise stated.

Chain-4 at beginning of round counts as first double crochet and chain-1 unless otherwise stated.

Chain-5 at beginning of round counts as first double crochet and chain-2 unless otherwise stated.

Chain-7 at beginning of round or row counts as first treble crochet and chain-3 unless otherwise stated.

Weave in ends as work progresses.

Special Stitches

4-double crochet cluster (4-dc cl): Yo, insert hook in indicated st or sp, yo, pull up a lp, yo, draw through 2 lps on hook *(2 lps on hook)*, [yo, insert hook in same st or sp, yo and pull up a lp, yo, draw through 2 lps] 3 times *(5 lps on hook)*, yo, draw through all 5 lps on hook *(see illustration)*.

Double Crochet Cluster

5-double crochet cluster (5-dc cl): Yo, insert hook in indicated st or sp, yo, pull up a lp, yo, draw through 2 lps on hook *(2 lps on hook)*, [yo, insert hook in same st or sp, yo and pull up a lp, yo, draw through 2 lps] 4 times *(6 lps on hook)*, yo, draw through all 6 lps on hook.

2-treble cluster (2-tr cl): *Yo 2 times, insert hook in indicated st, yo, pull up a lp, [yo, draw through 2 lps] 2 times, rep from *, yo, draw through all 3 lps on hook.

Large fan (lg fan): ([Dc, ch 1] 4 times, dc) in indicated st or sp.

V-stitch (V-st): (Dc, ch 1, dc) in indicated st or sp.

Small fan (sm fan): ([Dc, ch 1] 3 times, dc) in indicated st or sp.

Changing Colors

Color changes use the **chain change color** *(see StitchGuide.com)* technique unless otherwise indicated.

For solid-colored motifs, disregard instructions to change colors.

Throw

Hexagon Motif 1

Make 9 multicolor motifs and 3 solid-color motifs in each of colors A, B and C.

Rnd 1: With A, make a **slip ring** *(see illustration)*, **ch 3** *(see Pattern Notes)*, 17 dc in ring, **join** *(see Pattern Notes)* in top of beg ch-3, pull tail to close ring. *(18 dc)*

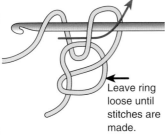

Leave ring loose until stitches are made.

Slip Ring

Rnd 2: Ch 1, sc in same st as join, [ch 3, sk next 2 dc, sc in next dc] 5 times, ch 3, join in first sc, fasten off. *(6 sc, 6 ch-3 sps)*

Rnd 3: With B *(see Changing Colors)*, sl st in first ch-3 sp, ch 1 (sc, hdc, 3 dc, hdc, sc) in each ch-3 sp around, join in first sc, fasten off. *(12 sc, 12 hdc, 18 dc)*

Rnd 4: With C, (**ch 7**–*see Pattern Notes*, tr) in first sc, [ch 2, sk next 2 sts, sc in next dc, ch 2, sk next 3 sts, (tr, ch 3, tr) in next sc] 5 times, ch 2, sk next 2 sts, ch

2, join in 4th ch of beg ch-7. *(6 sc, 12 tr, 12 ch-2 sps, 6 ch-3 sps)*

Rnd 5: Ch 1, [5 sc in next ch-3 sp, sk next tr, 2 sc in next ch-2 sp, ch 2, sk next sc, 2 sc in next ch-2 sp, sk next tr] 6 times, join in first sc, fasten off. *(54 sc, 6 ch-2 sps)*

Rnd 6: With A, ch 3, dc in next sc, [**V-st** *(see Special Stitches)* in next sc, dc in next 4 sc, dc in next ch-2 sp, dc in next 4 sc] 5 times, V-st in next sc, dc in next 4 sc, dc in next ch-2 sp, dc in last 2 sc, join in top of beg ch-3, fasten off. *(66 dc, 6 ch-1 sps)*

Hexagon Motif 2

Make 9 multicolor motifs and 3 solid-color motifs in each of colors A, B and C.

Rnd 1: With C, make a slip ring, ch 1, 12 sc in ring, join in first sc, pull tail to close ring. *(12 sc)*

Rnd 2: Ch 1, sc in first sc, [ch 3, sk next sc, sc in next sc] 5 times, ch 3, join in first sc, fasten off. *(6 sc, 6 ch-3 sps)*

Rnd 3: With A, ch 1, sl st in first ch-3 sp, ch 3, **4-dc cl** *(see Special Stitches)* in same sp *(counts as first 5-dc cl)*, [ch 6, sk next sc, **5-dc cl** *(see Special Stitches)* in next ch-3 sp] 5 times, ch 6, join in first 4-dc cl, fasten off. *(6 5-dc cls, 6 ch-6 sps)*

Rnd 4: With C, ch 1, sc in same st as join, [3 sc in next ch-6 sp, working in front of ch-6, tr in next sc 2 rnds below, 3 sc in same ch-6 sp as last sc made*, sc in next 5-dc cl] around, ending last rep at *, join in first sc, fasten off. *(6 tr, 42 sc)*

Rnd 5: With B, ch 3, dc in next 3 sc, [V-st in next tr, dc in next 7 sc] 5 times, V-st in next tr, dc in last 3 sc, join in top of beg ch-3, fasten off. *(54 dc, 6 ch-1 sps)*

Rnd 6: With A, ch 3, dc in next 4 dc, V-st in next ch-1 sp, [dc in next 9 dc, V-st in next ch-1 sp] 5 times, V-st in next ch-1 sp, dc in last 4 dc, join in top of beg ch-3, fasten off. *(66 dc, 6 ch-1 sps)*

Hexagon Motif 3

Make 9 multicolor motifs and 3 solid-color motifs in each of colors A, B and C.

Rnd 1: With B, make a slip ring, ch 3, 2 dc in ring, ch 2, [3 dc, ch 2 in ring] 3 times, join in top of beg ch-3, fasten off. *(12 dc, 4 ch-2 sps)*

Rnd 2: With C, ch 1, sc in same st as join, sc in next 2 dc, [3 sc in next ch-2 sp, sc in next 3 dc] 3 times, 3 sc in last ch-2 sp, join in first sc, fasten off. *(24 sc)*

Rnd 3: With A, ch 3, dc in next 3 sc, ch 3, [dc in next 4 sc, ch 3] 5 times, join in top of beg ch-3. *(24 dc, 6 ch-3 sps)*

Rnd 4: Ch 5 *(see Pattern Notes)*, [sk next 2 dc, dc in next dc, (2 dc, ch 1, 2 dc) in next ch-3 sp, dc in next dc, ch 2] 5 times, sk next 2 dc, dc in next dc, (2 dc, ch 1, 2 dc) in last ch-3 sp, join in 3rd ch of beg ch-5, fasten off. *(36 dc, 6 ch-2 sps, 6 ch-1 sps)*

Rnd 5: With C, ch 1, sc in same st as join, [2 sc in next ch-2 sp, sc in next 3 dc, 2 sc in next ch-1 sp, sc in next 3 dc] 5 times, 2 sc in next ch-2 sp, sc in next 3 dc, 2 sc in next ch-1 sp, sc in last 2 dc, join in first sc, fasten off. *(60 sc)*

Rnd 6: With B, ch 3, dc in next 6 sc, [V-st in next sc, dc in next 9 sc] 5 times, V-st in next sc, sc in last 2 sts, join in top of beg ch-3, fasten off. *(66 dc, 6 ch-1 sps)*

Hexagon Motif 4

Make 9 multicolor motifs and 3 solid-color motifs in each of colors A, B and C.

Rnd 1: With A, ch 7, join in first ch to form a ring, ch 1, 12 sc in ring, join in first sc, fasten off. *(12 sc)*

Rnd 2: With B, **ch 4** *(see Pattern Notes)*, dc in same st as join, V-st in each sc around, join in 3rd ch of beg ch-4, fasten off. *(24 dc, 12 ch-1 sps)*

Rnd 3: With A, sl st in first ch-1 sp, ch 4, tr in same sp *(counts as first 2-tr cl)*, [ch 4, sk next 2 dc, **2-tr cl** *(see Special Stitches)* in next ch-1 sp] 11 times, ch 4, join in top of first 2-tr cl, fasten off. *(12 2-tr cl, 12 ch-4 sps)*

Rnd 4: With B, sl st in next ch-4 sp, ch 1, 5 sc in each ch-4 sp around, join in first sc, fasten off. *(60 sc)*

Rnd 5: With C, ch 3, dc in next 4 sc, [V-st in next sc, dc in next 9 sc] 5 times, V-st in next st, dc in last 4 sc, join in top of beg ch-3, fasten off. *(66 dc, 6 ch-1 sps)*

Half-Hexagon Motif

Make 10.

Row 1 (RS): With A, make a slip ring, ch 1, 7 sc in ring, pull end to close ring, do not join in first sc, turn. *(7 sc)*

Row 2: Ch 1, sc in first sc, [ch 3, sk next sc, sc in next sc] 3 times, turn. *(4 sc, 3 ch-3 sps)*

Row 3: Ch 7, [5-dc cl in next ch-3 sp, ch 3, tr in next sc, ch 3] 2 times, ch 3, 5-dc cl in last ch-3 sp, ch 3, tr in last sc, turn. *(4 tr, 3 5-dc cls, 6 ch-3 sps)*

Row 4: Ch 1, sc in first tr, [3 sc in next ch-3 sp, sc in next 5-dc cl, 3 sc in next ch-3 sp, sc in next tr] 2 times, 3 sc in next ch-3 sp, sc in next tr, 3 sc in ch-3 sp of beg ch-7, sc in 4th ch of beg ch-7, turn. *(25 sc)*

Row 5: Ch 3, [dc in next 7 sc, V-st in next sc] 2 times, dc in last 8 sc, turn. *(27 dc, 2 ch-1 sps)*

Row 6: Ch 3, dc in same st as ch-3, [dc in each dc to next ch-1 sp, V-st in next ch-1 sp] 2 times, dc in each dc to last dc, 2 dc in last dc, fasten off. *(33 dc, 2 ch-1 sps)*

Assembly

Arrange Motifs with RS facing up. Refer to **Assembly Diagram** *(see Assembly Diagram)* for placement of motifs and strips.

With a length of A 3 times longer than seams to be joined, join Motifs into 11 strips using **invisible seam** *(see illustration)* or your preferred method. Use same method to join strips tog.

Invisible Seam

Finishing

Border

Rnd 1: Join A in corner ch-1 sp of first hexagon in Strip 1 *(see star in Assembly Diagram, all border rnds will start at this location on blanket)*, ch 1, (sc, ch 1, sc) in same sp as join, *sc in next 11 dc, [(sc, ch 1, sc) in next ch-1 sp, sc in next 10 dc, **sc dec** (see StitchGuide.com) over next 2 dc, sc in next 10 dc] 6 times, (sc, ch 1, sc) in next ch-1 sp, dc in next 11 sc, (sc, ch 1, sc) in next ch-1 sp, rotate to work 187 sc evenly across long edge to next ch-1 sp, (sc, ch 1, sc) in next ch-1 sp, rep from *, join in first sc. *(164 sc on each short side, 189 sc on each long side, 18 ch-1 sps)*

Rnd 2: Ch 3, V-st in next ch-1 sp, dc in each sc to next ch-1 sp, *[V-st in next ch-1 sp, dc in next 10 sc, **dc dec** (see StitchGuide.com) over next 3 sc, dc in next 10 sc] 6 times, [V-st in next ch-1 sp, dc in each sc to next ch-1 sp] 3 times, rep from * around, ending last rep with dc in each rem sc, join in top of beg ch-3. *(168 dc on each short side, 191 dc on each long side, 18 ch-1 sps)*

Rnd 3: Sl st in next dc, sl st in next ch-1 sp, ch 4, ([dc, ch 1] 3 times, dc) in same ch sp *(counts as first lg fan)*, place marker in center dc of fan, *[sk next 3 dc, sc in next dc, sk next 3 dc, **lg fan** (see Special Stitches) in next dc, sk next 3 dc, sc in next dc, sk next 3 dc, lg fan in next ch-1 sp, sk next 3 dc, sc in next dc, sk next 3 dc, lg fan in next dc, sk next 3 dc** sc in next dc] 7 times, ending last rep at **, lg fan in next ch-1 sp, place marker in center dc of last fan made, [sk next 3 dc, sc in next dc, sk next 3 dc, lg fan in next dc] across to 7 sts before next ch-1 sp, sk next 3 dc, sc in next dc, sk next 3 dc*** lg fan in next ch-1 sp, place marker in center dc of last fan made, rep from * ending last rep at ***, join in 3rd ch of beg ch-4, fasten off. *(92 sc, 92 lg fans)*

Rnd 4: Join D in first marked dc after join at end of last rnd, ch 1, (sc, ch 1, sc) in same dc as join, *[ch 2, V-st in next sc, ch 2**, sc in center dc of next lg fan] 2 times, ending last rep at **, (sc, ch 1, sc) in center dc of next lg fan, rep between [ ] 3 times, ending last

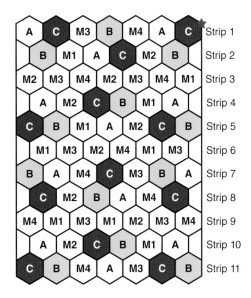

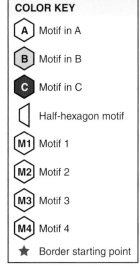

Ionian Hexagon Tile Throw
Assembly Diagram

rep at ** across to next marker, (sc, ch 1, sc) in marked dc, rep between [ ] to next marked dc, (sc, ch 1, sc) in marked dc, rep from * around, ending last rep at **, join in first sc. *(110 sc, 92 V-sts)*

Rnd 5: Ch 1, sc in first sc, **sm fan** (see Special Stitches) in next ch-1 sp, place marker in center ch-1 sp of sm fan just made, *sc in next sc, [lg fan in next V-st, sc in next sc] 2 times, sm fan in next ch-1 sp, {sc in next sc, rep between [ ] 3 times, sm fan in next ch-1 sp} 6 times, sc in next sc, rep between [ ] 2 times, sm fan in next ch-1 sp, sc in next sc, rep between [ ] across to next ch-1 sp, rep from * around, join in first sc, fasten off. *(110 sc, 92 lg fans, 18 sm fans)*

Rnd 6: Join E in marked ch-1 sp, ch 1, (sc, ch 1, sc) in same sp as join, *[ch 2, V-st in next sc, ch 2**, sc in center dc of next lg fan] around to next sm fan, ending last rep at **, (sc, ch 1, sc) in center ch-1 sp of next sm fan, place marker in ch-1 sp just made, rep from * around, ending last rep at **, join in first sc. *(128 sc, 110 V-sts)*

Rnd 7: Ch 1, sc in first sc, *{sm fan in next ch-1 sp, sc in next sc, [sm fan in next V-st, sc in next sc] around to next ch-1 sp} around to next marked ch-1 sp, sm fan in marked ch-1 sp, sc in next sc, [lg fan in next V-st**, sc in next sc] around to next marked ch-1 sp, rep from * around, ending last rep at **, join in first sc, fasten off. ●

Metric Conversion Charts

METRIC CONVERSIONS

yards	x	.9144	=	meters (m)
yards	x	91.44	=	centimeters (cm)
inches	x	2.54	=	centimeters (cm)
inches	x	25.40	=	millimeters (mm)
inches	x	.0254	=	meters (m)

centimeters	x	.3937	=	inches
meters	x	1.0936	=	yards

INCHES INTO MILLIMETERS & CENTIMETERS (Rounded off slightly)

inches	mm	cm	inches	cm	inches	cm	inches	cm
1/8	3	0.3	5	12.5	21	53.5	38	96.5
1/4	6	0.6	5 1/2	14	22	56	39	99
3/8	10	1	6	15	23	58.5	40	101.5
1/2	13	1.3	7	18	24	61	41	104
5/8	15	1.5	8	20.5	25	63.5	42	106.5
3/4	20	2	9	23	26	66	43	109
7/8	22	2.2	10	25.5	27	68.5	44	112
1	25	2.5	11	28	28	71	45	114.5
1 1/4	32	3.2	12	30.5	29	73.5	46	117
1 1/2	38	3.8	13	33	30	76	47	119.5
1 3/4	45	4.5	14	35.5	31	79	48	122
2	50	5	15	38	32	81.5	49	124.5
2 1/2	65	6.5	16	40.5	33	84	50	127
3	75	7.5	17	43	34	86.5		
3 1/2	90	9	18	46	35	89		
4	100	10	19	48.5	36	91.5		
4 1/2	115	11.5	20	51	37	94		

KNITTING NEEDLES CONVERSION CHART

Canada/U.S.	0	1	2	3	4	5	6	7	8	9	10	10½	11	13	15
Metric (mm)	2	2¼	2¾	3¼	3½	3¾	4	4½	5	5½	6	6½	8	9	10

CROCHET HOOKS CONVERSION CHART

Canada/U.S.	1/B	2/C	3/D	4/E	5/F	6/G	7	8/H	9/I	10/J	10½/K	N
Metric (mm)	2.25	2.75	3.25	3.5	3.75	4	4.5	5	5.5	6	6.5	9.0

Annie's® Published by Annie's, 306 East Parr Road, Berne, IN 46711. Printed in USA. Copyright © 2024 Annie's. All rights reserved. This publication may not be reproduced in part or in whole without written permission from the publisher.

RETAIL STORES: If you would like to carry this publication or any other Annie's publication, visit AnniesWSL.com.

Every effort has been made to ensure that the instructions in this publication are complete and accurate. We cannot, however, take responsibility for human error, typographical mistakes or variations in individual work. Please visit AnniesCustomerService.com to check for pattern updates.

ISBN: 979-8-89253-303-4

1 2 3 4 5 6 7 8 9